THE DECLINE OF CAPITALISM

THE DECLINE OF CAPITALISM

The Economics of a Period of the Decline of Capitalism After Stabilisation

Eugen Varga

The Decline of Capitalism: *The Economics of a Period of the Decline of Capitalism After Stabilisation*
Eugen Varga

First Published, 1928
First Indian Edition, 2012

ISBN 978-93-5002-182-8 (Hb)

Published by
AAKAR BOOKS
28 E Pocket IV, Mayur Vihar Phase I, Delhi 110 091
Phone : 011 2279 5505 Telefax : 011 2279 5641
aakarbooks@gmail.com; www.aakarbooks.com

Printed at
Arpit Printographers, Delhi 110 032
arpitprinto@yahoo.com

Contents

Foreword

The object of this work is to give, in a very small space, a sketch of the most important facts and tendencies within capitalism in decline, in the last few years, since stabilisation. It does not claim to be exhaustive. Many very important theoretical problems are omitted, such as the question of the *determination of prices in the post-war period*; why, in spite of the increased productivity and intensity of labour, in spite of the decrease in the production of gold, involving no considerable decrease in the cost of production of gold—why is the price level 50 per cent higher than before the war? An answer to this question would require a detailed analysis of the prices of different commodities on the one hand, and, on the other, the reopening of the old dispute concerning the influence on prices of the cost of the production of gold, and what, taking into account the varied gold content of ore and the variations in the cost of production, actually determines its value. Such a discussion must be reserved for a later and purely theoretical work; the theoretical analysis of the form of capitalist economy with a monetary unit changing, and not constant, in value (*Theory of the economics of inflation and deflation*). But there are a number of important problems which are *general problems of capitalism, and which, at the present time, show no particular characteristics*, either not dealt with at all or only touched upon lightly, such as the problem of the desultory development of capitalism. In the present work we shall confine ourselves to those problems, politically the most important, which are characteristic of the present period; to the facts which demonstrate that the stabilisation of capitalism does not mean the stability of the capitalist system; that the internal contradictions of stabilised capitalism must necessarily lead to new revolutionary situations, that the *period of the decline of capitalism is not ended.....*

In order to assist the reader I have maintained the following plan: the text itself contains the actual examination of the subject and the most important data; the footnotes contain references and supplementary figures and data; and, finally, the Appendix contains the complete tables which are essential to any reader who wishes to become thoroughly acquainted with the statistical bases of this work. I believe that this arrangement will enable readers, and, above all, the workers, to master this publication. It was not, of course, possible to remove all difficulties; the subject itself is too complicated for that. The reader will have to resign himself to reading a few chapters through twice...

Eugen Varga
Moscow, June 1, 1928

1

The Stabilisation of Capitalism

The elemental revolt of the masses during and immediately after the war resulted in the complete overthrow of the capitalists in Russia, in the temporary loss of their power in Hungary, Finland, Bavaria; in capitalism being seriously endangered in all the belligerent European countries.

In that extremely dangerous situation, the capitalists executed a sham retreat all along the line; submitting to the pressure of the masses, they seemed willing to surrender power to the workers or to share it with them. They made enormous sacrifices in order to maintain the capitalist system. In a few countries they even ceased for a while to exploit in order to save the conditions necessary for exploitation, their class supremacy. They resigned from government in favour of the reformist Labour leaders; all the customary *political* working class demands were satisfied— abolition of the monarchy and upper chamber; universal, equal and secret franchise for all political institutions, freedom of meeting and association, liberty of the press, etc. Similarly with the old *social* demands— the eight-hour day, general social insurance, work found for all demobilised soldiers, rights of the workers in the factories (factory councils), etc. The capitalists were most accommodating with regard to wages also. They pacified the revolt of the masses by setting up "Nationalisation Commissions," by sham preparations for agrarian reform. *The capitalists had, at any price, to gain time in order to re-establish their crumbling machinery of power and to give the reformists the opportunity of guiding the elemental revolt of the working masses into "orthodox channels."*

We wish to emphasise here—in order to avoid any misunderstanding—that we are describing the historical significance, the meaning of events, and not what actually occurred in the immediate consciousness of individual persons. The capitalists, individually, recoiled from the proletarian revolt, for they had neither the courage nor the power to face it boldly. Only a few leading politicians were clearly conscious of the fact that *the bourgeoisie as a class had effected a sham retreat of historical importance*; but that does not affect the significance of events.

The capitalist retreat manoeuvre was crowned with complete success. The great mass of workers believed the statement of the reformists that a victorious and bloodless revolution had occurred. They did not realise that the outward appearances lacked a *class* content; that although the reformist leaders were ruling, the workers were, not in power. The basis of capitalism, private ownership of the means of production, was not touched. The bourgeois State-machine, shaken by defeat, was not destroyed, but renewed and strengthened by the assimilation of the reformist leaders who placed the working-class organisations, which supported them, at the service of the capitalists. What appeared to the workers as their victory—their leaders becoming Presidents, Ministers, Secretaries of State—was actually a victory for the capitalists. The leaders of the bourgeoisie and their reformist lackeys allied themselves together to prevent the social revolution, to avoid the dictatorship of the proletariat!

This sham retreat gave the capitalists what they most wanted—time! And they exploited it excellently. With the help of the reformists they assembled and reorganised the State machinery of force; where necessary, they created armed class troops on a Fascist basis. Assisted ideologically and organisationally by the reformists, and increasing from time to time the use of violence, they defeated the attempts of the revolutionary vanguard to transform the apparent victory of the workers into a real proletarian revolution. *As, section by section, the workers were defeated, the concessions which the bourgeoisie had been compelled to grant at the end of the war in order to stem the tide of working-class revolt, were withdrawn*!

In this way, the possibility of realisation of capital was gradually regained. The capitalists of a few countries had already succeeded before this in realising their capital by means of inflation. *The historical function of inflation was to annul economically those concessions granted by the capitalists to the workers for political reasons, to prevent the social revolution.* Real wages were constantly falling. The material achievements gained by the workers were soon lost on the road of inflation. The capitalists expropriated the property of the rentiers, the petty bourgeoisie and the peasants; and, through inflation, they succeeded to some extent in transferring the burden of maintaining the workers on to the independent producers. With decreasing production the large-scale capitalists, by appropriating the surplus value again being created because of inflation, and by the consequent expropriation of the property of the middle classes, were enabled to enrich themselves. *The realisation of capital was restored by inflation, although upon an "abnormal," temporary and fluctuating basis.*[1]

But inflation is only a temporary method for realisation of capital, and one which is not suitable for the capitalists of all countries.[2] After having strengthened their position the bourgeoisie had to take up the direct struggle against the workers. And in this struggle they were victorious. Then followed the political *"stabilisation" of capitalism: the relation of forces between capitalists and workers had shifted so far in the favour of the former that struggles for power could for the moment no longer be taken up with any prospect of success.*

In internal policy this was evidenced by the fact that the capitalists ruled without the cooperation of the reformists. This afforded the reformists the opportunity of forming an opposition within the capitalist system, of conducting a struggle for the economic demands of the workers and, in this manner, of regaining to some extent the doubtful confidence of the workers. Such a state of affairs is advantageous to the bourgeoisie, for it enables the reformists to act more successfully as capitalist agents within the working class when any acutely revolutionary situation arises—so long as the bourgeoisie has not resorted to capitalist terror—to Fascism—as a system of government.

The capitalist victory was, by the reciprocal action of history, both conditioned by and the condition of the *economic* stabilisation of capitalism. The realisation of capital, the production and appropriation of surplus value, accumulation, is again proceeding normally. Exchanges are stable. National and international credit is again restored. The break-up of the capitalist world into two spheres of over-production and under-production, peculiarly characteristic of the post-war period, was slowly surmounted, the rich countries "supporting" the poor countries by means of capital exports.

Technical progress set in at a great rate. The machinery of production was rapidly renewed and extended. Production outstripped the level of the pre-war period.[3] The reformists foretold a new, long-enduring boom of capitalism, a growth, already in process of development, towards socialism by way of State capitalism, economic democracy, the cooperatives, small shareholdings, etc.[4] Post-war capitalism is leading to a peaceful *super-imperialism*, whose economic basis is international monopoly, economic cooperation between banks of issue and the balance of forces; whose form of organisation is the *League of Nations*. Later on we shall deal with this theory in greater detail. At this point we only wish to state the following:

It would be *blind stupidity to attempt to deny the fact of the economic and political stabilisation of capitalism* as compared with the position in the years immediately following the war. But it is equally incorrect to over-estimate the economic and political results of stabilisation.

Annual production in the capitalist countries of western Europe increased on the average by 3 per cent in the half century preceding the war. This is a very rough calculation, but it gives an approximately correct picture. For the period 1913-1928 this would correspond to an increase of about 50 per cent. Table II in the Appendix shows that the pre-war average has not by any means been reached. The waste of the war has not yet been replaced.[5]

The following, is, however, decisive.

As far as the *actual period of stabilisation* is concerned, the increase of production is significant. It would, however, be quite false to assume that this will be the normal rate of progress from now on; it is an exceptional state of affairs, conditioned by the intensity of the post-war crisis and by the fact that 1927 was for Germany (and for the first half of the year for the U.S.A. also) a year of good markets.

The following is, however, decisive.

Capitalism in the post-war period is no simple restoration of pre-war capitalism. It is a different capitalism.

It is no longer a "dying" capitalism, but one already in the process of mortification, which has lost a sixth part of the world, an important part of its former sphere of hegemony, to its grave-digger, the proletariat. And within the still existing capitalism those contradictions which are peculiar to it are rapidly growing sharper, and are heading straight for a new catastrophe. *The sharpening of these contradictions forms the actual theme of the rest of this work.*

NOTES

1. We wish to emphasise the fact that, in the given relation of class forces, inflation was economically inevitable. It was not

consciously arranged by the capitalists; but historically inflation served to accomplish the appropriation of surplus value indirectly, this being impossible directly.

2. Inflation was of no use to the British bourgeoisie because of the lack of a peasant class, and because of the great importance of international financial concerns. It would, by expropriating the rentier class, have brought the capitalists directly face to face with the workers, there being no peasantry to act as a protective buffer class. It would have meant the end of London as the world-banker.
3. *See Table I of Appendix: Figures of World Production.* This deals only with raw materials, since there are no statistics dealing with the production of finished goods. But it may be assumed that the production of finished goods increased in accordance with that of raw materials, and perhaps increased even more because of the improvements introduced in the utilisation of raw materials (fuel technique, utilisation of old materials, avoidance of waste). The table shows that the production of the most important raw materials outstripped that of the pre-war period, particularly metals.

   This is evidence of the extension in the machinery of production, and of great accumulation. The increase in the production of food and textiles scarcely keeps pace with the increase in population, which shows that the real standard of life of the people as a whole, and of the workers in particular, has not improved.
4. Hilferding writes: "...the extension of productive capacity means finally, [?] after crises have been overcome, an increase in production and new good markets. At the same time, the agrarian revolution means an extension of the market for industrial products." ("Problems of Today," "Die Gesellschaft," 1924, No. 1).
5. Taking the world production of coal and pig-iron as indicating

the general trend we get the following figures: (*a*)

	Coal Mill. tons	*Annual increases %*	*Pig-Iron mill. tons*		*Annual increase %*
1865	188	—	9.1		—
1875	283	5.05	14.1		5.60
1885	407	4.38	19.8		4.04
1895	583	4.35	29.4		4.84
1905	914	5.68	54.8		8.64
1913	1,242	4.45	77.2	(78.8) (b)	5.02
1921	1,030	–2.13		(37.8)	–6.50
1925	1,229	4.83		(76.9)	25.80
1927	1,300	2.90	85.0		5.42

(*a*) Figures up to 1905 taken from Cassel's "Social Economy,"1913, 1921 and 1925 from International Statistical Annual; 1927 estimated. Percentages calculated by the author.

(*b*) According to "Statistical Annual."

2

The Instability of the Capitalist System

Stabilisation is not synonymous with stability. Capitalism never was, and never can be, stable. In a society where the means of production and the actual producers are separated from each other, where the social connection of human beings appears as the material relation of commodities, where the destinies of men acting blindly for themselves are not made subject to conscious laws, where the great majority is governed and exploited by a diminishing minority—in such a society stability is impossible. It is essentially part of the capitalist system that its balance is unstable, its instability constant. In times of apparent stability, the elements of contradiction are unfolding uninterruptedly until they reach a violent solution in a crisis, and balance is for a moment restored.

> *"The crises are always but momentary and forcible solutions of the existing contradictions, violent eruptions which restore the disturbed equilibrium for a while."*
>
> —(Marx, *Capital*, Volume III, Section I., p. 292.)

A stable capitalism without crises is impossible. Marx protests against the idea that within the capitalist system of production there exists merely the possibility of crises, "as though it were accidental whether or not they occur,"[1] as though there could be any measures to prevent the periodic recurrence of crises. Why can there be no capitalist economy without crises? The answer to that is:[2]

> "The conditions of direct exploitation and those of the realisation of surplus value are not identical. They are separated logically as well as by time and space. The first are only limited by the productive power of society; the last by the proportional relations of the various lines of production and by the consuming power of society. This last-named power is not determined either by the absolute productive power nor by the absolute consuming power, but by the consuming power based on antagonistic conditions of distribution, which reduces the consumption of the great mass of the population to a variable minimum within more or less narrow limits. The consuming power is furthermore restricted by the tendency to accumulate, the greed for an expansion of capital and a production of surplus value on an enlarged scale. This is a law of capitalist production imposed by incessant revolutions in the methods of production themselves, the resulting depreciation of existing capital, the general competitive struggle and the necessity of improving the product and expanding the scale of production, for the sake of self-preservation and on penalty of failure."

These remarks apply with equal validity to present-day capitalism; the formation of national and international monopolies can mitigate the harmful consequences of crises for the capital concerned in those monopolies, as we shall show later, and can burden the workers and the independent producers with the full weight of the crisis. But this automatically leads to an intensification of the next crisis, for:

> "The last cause of all crises always remains the poverty and restricted consumption of the masses as compared to the tendency of capitalist production to develop the productive forces in such a way that only the absolute power of consumption of the entire society would be their limit."[3]

The formation of monopolies and rationalisation means,

however, a decrease in the proportion of variable capital to the yearly value of products, i.e., a decrease in the working-class share of the total value of the commodities, i.e., a still sharper operation of the "last cause."

Balance in the capitalist system itself was again and again restored for a time by an extension of the capitalist market. This occurred through the separation of industry and agriculture,[4] through the change of independent producers cultivating their own land into either wage-earners or small-scale capitalists; and through the peaceful or violent transportation of the capitalist system of production to foreign countries. In this way capitalist society, in spite of the periodically recurring crises, maintained itself as a system.

Bukharin writes on this point as follows:[5]

> "The crisis never goes beyond the limits of unsettling the system. Having concluded our examination we see the *system*, moving, fluctuating; but through all the movements and disturbances the balance is again and again restored."

The fundamental, world-historical difference between all previous crises of capitalism, and that which came to a head in the world war, consists in this, that previous crises did for a moment restore the balance of the capitalist system, *did succeed in solving the contradictions, although by force and with the most violent convulsion, it is true, yet still within the framework of the capitalist system, while this crisis led to the break up of the system itself, to the overthrow of the bourgeoisie and the attainment of the proletarian dictatorship in one of the greatest States of the world.*

The overthrow of the capitalist system and the establishment of the dictatorship of the proletariat within the Soviet Union signifies the beginning of the period of the decline of capitalism, the first ten years of which have already passed, of the historic period of the transition from capitalism to socialism through a series of successful and unsuccessful proletarian revolutions.

The destruction of the Russian bourgeoisie and the erection of the proletarian dictatorship exercise a powerful influence both on the economic substructure and on the political and ideological superstructure of the rest of the world. This influence can be summed up as follows: *the existence of the proletarian dictatorship in the Soviet Union intensifies all the contradictions in the rest of the world and strengthens all those forces which made possible the defeat of the bourgeoisie in Russia itself.*

Economic sub-structure: The possibility of overcoming crises by an extension of the capitalist market is limited by the boundaries of the Soviet Union, embracing as it does one-sixth of the earth. This means an intensification of economic crises; increased difficulty in overcoming them temporarily; sharpening of the internal contradictions of capitalism; lessened stability of the entire system. It means a new impetus towards a new re-division of the world.

Social-political superstructure: The downfall of the Russian bourgeoisie raises the class-consciousness of the proletariat, strengthens its readiness for struggle: it demonstrates the possibility of overthrowing capitalist class domination throughout the world; demonstrates that capitalism is not an eternal, but merely a historically- transitory form of society.

In the same way the overthrow of the bourgeoisie in Russia affects the opposition offered by the colonial and semi-colonial peoples to imperialist oppression. The Soviet Union is the rallying point of all anti-capitalist forces within capitalism, and this forms a new element of instability.

These effects are intensified by the demonstration, not merely of the possibility of overthrowing the bourgeoisie, but also of the fact that the capitalists are not essential for the management of the productive forces concerned in capitalism. The economy of the Soviet Union is developing at a more rapid rate since the conclusion of the civil war than that of the capitalist world.[6]

The political reaction of the existence of the Soviet Union, which exacerbates the social struggles in the capitalist world, is of a twofold character. In imperialist countries the recreation and strengthening of a labour aristocracy (U.S.A.); in second-class capitalist countries where the economic basis for a labour aristocracy is lacking, organised terror of the bourgeoisie—Fascism (Italy). In many cases both tendencies are apparent.

It is particularly significant of the present period of decline that parliamentary democracy, the form of government for which the rising bourgeoisie struggled against feudalism and which embodies capitalist political ideology, is decaying. Even before the war parliamentary democracy had, because of the concentration of capital and the formation of monopolies, become merely a caricature of itself. But the bourgeoisie held on to it as the most suitable means of awakening in the masses the illusion of their participation in power. Today the parliamentary system is legally abolished in Italy and Spain, and practically abolished in Poland and Portugal; in the Balkan countries it exists only as a sham (there are no legal Communist Parties). But even in those countries where the parliamentary regime still exists the idea of Fascism, the idea of capitalist terror, gains new adherents daily.[7]

Whence comes this change?

Parliamentary democracy serves as the State form of the bourgeoisie as long as it is a historically progressing class, as long as it can claim to serve the interests of the people as a whole. The Fascist State, organised terror in the interests of the capitalists, is the form of government adapted to the period of decline, when the rule of the bourgeoisie is seriously threatened. At the present time, since a mere handful of the greatest capitalists at the head of powerful monopoly organisations dominate economic and political life, since the class struggle has torn the democratic mask into shreds, the idea of Parliamentarism has lost its power. Its place is taken by the idea of Fascism, of unbridled nationalism, the final attempt to bind the petty bourgeois masses to capitalism; the proletariat—apart from the labour aristocracy—will no longer be bound to capitalism by any idea whatever. The white terror is taking the place of ideological domination. In the period of decline the bourgeoisie is losing its ideological leadership of the people....

In the sphere of foreign policy the instability of the system becomes increasingly obvious. There is no end to the palaver about eternal peace, disarmament and courts of arbitration, but military preparations on land, on sea, under the sea and in the air continue to be made uninterruptedly and hastily. There have never been military preparations on such a scale as those taking place today. Alliances and counter-alliances which change from day to day, blocs and counter-blocs, herald the coming war. The capitalists of certain countries (Italy, Germany, Hungary) publicly and brutally propose the question of the re-division of the world. The following main tendencies can be discerned in the general confusion:

(*a*) *The capitalist world against the Soviet Union*: As a hostile class, the bourgeoisie of the whole world is pursuing a common fight against the victorious proletariat of the Soviet Union.

(*b*) *Imperialist Powers against the colonial peoples*: The capitalists of all imperialist Powers have a common interest in maintaining their rule over the exploited colonial peoples. And since the Soviet Union is the natural leader of all anti-imperialist and anti-capitalist struggles the interests of the capitalist class in maintaining its supremacy against the workers in the home country are bound up with its interests in maintaining its domination of the oppressed peoples in the colonies, both coming to a head in a systematic preparation for war against the Soviet Union.

(*c*) Capitalism is not, however, a unified whole but is broken up into separate States each carrying on a struggle for its share of the world. Antagonisms among the imperialist States themselves prevent unified procedure. There is unity of principle in our camp because we have a common object, but the capitalist camp is split again and again by imperialist antagonisms. The bourgeoisie of the United States—which will later become the acknowledged leader of the anti-revolutionary struggle because of its position as the strongest capitalist Power— does not yet feel itself directly threatened by the proletarian revolution. Its own colonial sphere, Central and South America, lies far from the Soviet Union, and is less subject to the influence of the Soviet Union for economic and cultural reasons, than the Asiatic colonies of England. Hostility towards the two other imperialist world Powers—Britain and Japan—is at the present time still stronger than that towards the U.S.S.R. Britain's attempt to unite the European States into one bloc against the U.S.S.R. brings to light all the hidden antagonisms in the Balkans, in eastern and central Europe. The capitalists of the countries immediately bordering on the Soviet Union hesitate to enter upon war, for they realise that defeat would mean the immediate overthrow of their supremacy....

All these factors are indicative of extreme instability in all matters of foreign policy, and therefore in the whole system. Apart from the ever intensifying hostility between the two strongest imperialist Powers—the United States and Britain, apart from the "friendship" between England and France forced on them by the military situation,[8] everything is unstable, everything is continually changing. But all the Powers, without any exception, are arming themselves for a new war against each other.

This accounts for the irresolution of the bourgeoisie in the fight against the Soviet Union. The capitalists of the world, split by internal dissensions, *hesitate* to make the attack. Meanwhile imperialist antagonisms become more biter, the anti-capitalist and anti-imperialist forces within the bourgeois world increase and organise themselves, the U.S.S.R.'s capacity for defence grows with the progress of industrialisation. All this *forces* the world bourgeoisie to begin the attack...

Ideologically, the decline of capitalism is completely

manifest. The bourgeoisie *no longer possess a political ideology*. The old catchwords of liberty, equality, faternity are buried. The free trade ideology ekes out a precarious existence, for the bourgeoisie of each country demands protective tariffs for itself and free trade in other countries. The political ideology of the American bourgeoisie has been discredited by the tremendous unemployment and the misery of the independent producers; the nationalist-chauvinist ideology of Fascism by the capitalist terror.[9] *The economic theory of capitalism* today goes back even further than Ricardo; its most prominent representatives altogether deny the necessity for a theory of value, and disown the old bourgeois classical economists, because their theories lead directly to Marxism, to the doctrine of the historically transitory character of capitalism. No, longer Sombart, infected with Marxism, but Cassel, the most superficial vulgar economist, is the "leading theoretician of today." Marxism is strictly prohibited.[10]

Now, as before, the reformists call themselves Marxists. But reformist economic thought today contains not the smallest grain of Marxism. It is an extraordinary mixture of bourgeois twaddle (proposals for rationalisation, increase in labour productivity) and Sismondism (Capitalists should pay higher wages in order to be able to sell more goods).[11]

Summing up:

Instead of the stability and super-imperialism foretold by the reformists, we see the greatest disintegration, the greatest instability in capitalism today, both in its economic sub-structure and in its political-social and ideological super structure. The contradictions are becoming sharper and are making straight for a new imperialist war, either of the imperialists against the Soviet Union or of the imperialists among themselves, to determine the re-division of the world (a combination of both is possible).

NOTES

1. "Theories of Surplus Value," Volume II., p. 287 (German edition).
2. "Capital," Volume 3, Section II, p. 286.
3. Capital Vol. 3, p. 568.
4. "...only the destruction of rural domestic industry can give the internal market of a country that extension and consistence which the capitalist mode of production requires." ("Capital," Vol. I, p. 772.)
5. "The Period of Transformation," p. 109.
6. See Tables IV-VIII in Appendix.
7. It is significant of the decline of Parliamentarianism that, in the last elections in Germany, only 12 million took the trouble to vote, out of an electorate of 42 million.
8. France, by means of long-distance artillery, submarines and aircraft, holds England in check; while, with her superior naval force, England holds France in check by the threat to deprive her of her colonies.
9. The youth of the colonial bourgeoisie, educated in the universities of Europe and America, is seeking in vain for a revolutionary bourgeois ideology corresponding to their class. Nothing is left for them but to employ Marxism as the basis of their struggle against imperialism (which, were the struggle to change from being merely anti-imperialist into being anti-capitalist, they would certainly betray without any qualms). Thus, e.g. we see Chiang Kai Shek justifying the murder of Chinese Communists in "Marxist" words.
10. The following extracts are typical:
    "It is obvious that with this recognition of the complete and fundamental inadequacy of Ricardo's theory of costs, the caricature of it—the Socialist theory of value–proves useless and *we will not waste any time on the hair-splitting of its defenders.*" (Cassel: "Theory of Social Economy." Vol. I, p. 294. Emphasis ours.)

    Another luminary of present-day bourgeois economics, Keynes, regards Marxism, with the helplessness of a child:

    "....But Marxian socialism must always remain a portent to the historians of opinion —how a doctrine so illogical and so dull can have exercised so powerful and enduring an

influence over the minds of men, and through them, the events of history." (J.M. Keynes, "The End of Laissez-Faire," p. 34.)
The American political economists make no mention of Marx at all.

11. Tarnov's new pamphlet, "Why be Poor?" is typical of reformist ideology. ("Why be Poor?") Berlin, 1928.)

3

The Sharpening of Internal Contradictions: The Widespread Unemployment

"We have developed a fairly definite idea that an employer's business is to eliminate work."[1]

The fact of chronic mass unemployment in the post-war period is generally acknowledged. We were inclined to treat it merely as the consequence of the serious disturbances experienced by world economy—industrialisation of the transatlantic countries, impoverishment of Europe, and agrarian crises. These factors certainly are contributory causes. But a thorough examination of recent developments shows that the cause of this chronic mass unemployment does not lie primarily in those disturbances, but is a necessary result of the sharpening of the internal contradictions of capitalism. The nature of this contradiction is as follows:

Surplus value, in which the capitalists share, in accordance with definite laws, in proportion to their respective capital, is produced by the workers exploited by industrial capital. By industrial capital we understand, as Marxists, capital which, in its circulation, passes through the cycle of production, assuming and discarding the forms:

$M - C\frac{L}{\text{M. Prod.}}$ Production—C—M.[2] That is, productive capital invested in agriculture, industry, mining and transport. It is true that trading capital, financial capital, and loan capital exploit their workers, but the workers so employed do not directly create surplus value; their wages are a part of the apparent costs of the capitalist system of production. All profit, all income from sources other than labour, whatever the legal title of its sources may be, is a part of the surplus value appropriated by industrial capital. The total amount of profit is equal to the total amount of surplus value. Consequently the more workers who are being exploited at a certain rate of surplus value, the greater the mass of surplus value and the mass of profit.

The internal contradiction of the capitalist system of production consists in this, that although total profit equals total surplus value, each individual capitalist concern is constantly endeavouring to reduce the number of workers which it exploits, to replace human labour by machines, to reduce the total of surplus value.

For the capitalists, who have no insight into the nature of capitalist economy, and regard everything through the spectacles of competition, expenditure on the wages of labour forms an element of cost differing in no way from other elements of cost, fuel, raw materials, machinery, etc. Consequently as soon as the opportunity of reducing the costs of production arises machines are brought in to supplant the worker, the workers are thrown on to the scrap-heap, and the surplus value yielded is decreased. *The interests of the individual capitalist concern to assure to itself a larger share of total profit by reducing its individual costs of production through decreasing wage costs, are therefore in opposition for the interest of the class in having as high a realisation as possible of total capital...*[3]

This fact is responsible for three main tendencies in capitalism:

(*i*) The tendency to raise the organic composition in capital;

(*ii*) the tendency to a falling rate of profit[4]

(*iii*) the tendency to a diminishing number of workers.

At this juncture we shall only deal with the last named. On this question Marx says:

> "The accumulation of capital, though originally appearing as its quantitative extension only, is effected, as we have seen, under a progressive qualitative change in its composition, under a constant, increase of its constant, at the expense of its variable constituent....
>
> "Since the demand for labour is determined not by the amount of capital as a whole, but by its variable constituent alone, that demand falls progressively with the increase of the total capital, instead of ... rising in proportion to it. It falls relatively to the magnitude of the total capital, and at an accelerated rate as this magnitude increases....
>
> "With the growth of the total capital its variable constituent or the labour incorporated in it also does increase, but in a constantly diminishing proportion....The labouring population therefore produces, along with the accumulation of capital produced by it, the means by which itself is made relatively superfluous, is turned into a relative surplus population, and it does this to an always increasing extent. This is a law of population peculiar to the capitalist mode of production.... The greater the social wealth, the functioning capital, the extent and energy of its growth and, therefore, also the absolute mass of the proletariat and the productiveness of its labour, the greater is the industrial reserve army. The same causes which develop the expansive power of capital, develop also the labour power at its disposal. The relative mass of the industrial reserve army increases therefore with the potential energy of wealth."[5]

Up to the time of the world war it seemed as if this tendency, which theoretically must follow from the working of the capitalist system of production itself, did not apply to the sound capitalism of that time. It is true that the number of workers engaged in agriculture fell. But the number of those engaged productively in industry rose rapidly: when markets were favourable the industrial reserve army was absorbed, and complaints made of the lack of labour forces.[6]

This explains the popular belief—which Ricardo combatted so long ago—that the workers thrown on to the streets by the introduction of machines will *necessarily* find new opportunities for employment in production.[7]

In the post-war period, since the stabilisation of capitalism, a definite decrease in the number of workers employed by industrial capital—not only in agriculture—has taken place. The tendency towards making workers supernumerary is being completely worked out. *The displacement of workers by machinery is no longer compensated for by an extension of production.*[8]

This is such an important fact that we must demonstrate it carefully by figures and argument. First let us meet a possible objection: we are not here dealing with a phenomenon arising from the industrial cycle. We are not dealing with a decrease in the number of workers employed resulting from a decrease in the volume of production caused by a crisis: we are dealing with *unemployment at a time of good markets, of an increased volume of production, and in the leading capitalist countries*!

We shall first consider the United States. The following table shows the development of labour forces and of the volume of production since 1899[9].

	Workers employed in 1,000s		*Index for 1925 1899-100*		
	1899	*1925*	*Workers*	*Production*	*Production per worker*
Agriculture[10]	10,500	10,500	100	145	145
Mining	600	1,065	177	480	271
Industry	5,200	9,772	188	278	148
Railways	929	1,846	198	293	148
	17,229	23,183	135	247	183

This table is typical of development in the *former* capitalist epoch in the principal countries: an unchanging number of workers in agriculture, a great increase in industry, transport, and mining; but an increase in the volume of production of 147 per cent, corresponds to an increase in number of workers employed of 35 per cent. Production per worker increased by 83 per cent. *There is a relative displacement of labour power, for the increase in output per worker is less than the increase in the total volume of production. Hence the necessity for additional labour, power!*

Analysing the post-war period, we obtain an entirely different picture.

Development of labour forces and volume of production since 1919:[11]

	Workers employed in 1,000s		*Index for 1925 1899-100*		
	1899	*1925*	*Workers*	*Production*	*Production per worker*
Agriculture	11,300	10,500	93	108	118
Mining	1,065	1,065	100	133	133
Industry	10,689	9,772	91.5	128.5	140
Railways[12]	1,915	1,744	91	104.5	115
	24,969	23,081	93	120	129

We see that there is a decrease in labour employed of 7 per cent., but an increase in the volume of production of 20 per cent, and of production per worker of 29 per cent, *numerically a decrease of nearly two million. The increase in production per worker exceeds the extension of production. So labour power was completely dispensed with!*

The same process was clearly continued in the years 1926 and 1927; the census figures do not go beyond 1925, but the index figures of the Federal Reserve Board and of the Board of Labour will serve instead:

Index figures for factory industry

	1919	1920	1921	1922	1923	1924	1925	1926	1927
Production[13]	83	87	67	85	101	95	104	108	106
No. of workers[14]	—	—	85.1	88.4	100	90.3	91.2	91.9	88.2[15]

Finally we wish to show how, in particular industries, technical progress in recent years and rationalisation have caused stupendous unemployment.

The following tables give changes in American industry in 1923-27, and also the

(*a*) percentage changes in the volume of production;
(*b*) percentage changes in the number of workers;
(*c*) percentage changes in the demand for labour in relation to the volume of production (calculated on *a* and *b*).

	(*a*)	(*b*)	(*c*)
Refined petroleum	+84	–5	89
Tobacco	+53	–13	66
Meat slaughtering and packing	+20	–19	39
Railways (1922-26)	+30	–1	31
Automobiles	+69	+48	21
Motor tyres	+28	+7	21
Soft coal	+4	–15	19
Electricity (1922-27)	+70	+52	18
Steel	+8	–9	17
Agriculture (1920-5)	+10	–5	15
Cotton goods	+3	–13	16
Wood products	–6	–21	15
Men's clothing	+1	–7	8

This table shows that in five years the production per worker in the most important industries rose by about 20 per cent. How great is this progress is demonstrated by the fact that Sombart calculates the increase in the productivity of labour in industry for the entire "high capitalist" period, that is, for the 100 years preceding the war, to be merely 100 per cent. Progress has been made in the last five years which formerly took 20 years.[16]

The result of this development is gigantic unemployment increasing from year to year. This is accentuated by the normal increase in labour forces and by immigration. Graphs illustrating this development are given in the Appendix.

Figures for England show the same development.

The number of workers engaged in industry and transport amounted to, in thousands:[17]

	Beginning of 1923	*Beginning of 1928*	
Insured	9,701	8,992	–709
Unemployed	1,333	1,094	–239
Working	8,368	7,898	–470
Index of production[18]	88.7	96.3	+7.6

We see that the number of workers has decreased by about half a million, that is, 6 per cent, while the volume of production increased by 7.6 per cent. The tendency towards the creation of mass unemployment is clear, particularly if we take into account that there is an annual access of 200,000 new workers into the labour forces, and that some ten thousand are each year displaced in agriculture.[19] The statistics available for other countries do not suffice to demonstrate the origin of this widespread unemployment, but the fact of chronic mass unemployment in most European countries is enough to show that the same causes are also at work there.

Where are the workers thus thrown out of employment?

The figures for America and England show that a part of the workers no longer required by industrial capital, the number being increased by the natural growth in labour forces, does find employment elsewhere, otherwise the number of unemployed would be much greater than it is. The following calculation for the United States was made by Corey.[20] Between 1919 and 1926 there was, according to the figures of the National Bureau of Economic Research, an increase in the number of wage-earners of 4,312,000. Since, as a result of technical progress, there were 2,125,000 less workers employed by industrial capital, 6,500,000 persons were compelled to seek a livelihood outside agriculture, industry, transport and mining. Taking as his basis the increase between 1910 and 1920 in those branches of employment outside the sphere of industrial capital, and making certain additions thereto, the author calculates that of this 6,500,000, the numbers finding situations were as follows:

In commerce	1,000,000
Managers and officials (not in service of industrial capital)	1,000,000
Liberal professions	650,000
Motor trade and service	700,000
Public service	250,000
Various	350,000
Total	3,950,000

Apart from these, about 650,000 new workers found employment in the building trades, which, in any case, is within the sphere of industrial capital. We are then faced with the following results.

A decrease of about one and a half million in the number of workers directly creating surplus value in the service of industrial capital; an increase of about four millions in the number employed in distribution and various other services.[21] The capacity of the distribution services to absorb workers is of course a limited one, the whole course of development is abnormal. The rationalisation of trading and of all forms of office work also tends to decrease the amount of labour employed in this sphere. The contradiction between technical organisational progress, between the immense increase in social wealth, and the growing army of permanently unemployed, is the most powerful element of instability within the most stable capitalism, and it has tremendous social importance.

NOTES

1. R.C. Tugwell, "Industry's Coming of Age," New York, 1927, p. 27.
2. This is a formula expressing the circulation of capital through the process of production. Starting as money capital (M) it is turned into commodities (C), these commodities taking the form of labour power (L) and means of production (M. Prod.); the process of manufacture of production then takes place, resulting in the capital having been once more transformed into commodities; these are sold, and by their sale the capital (plus the surplus value created) is once more in the form of money.
3. The cheapening of commodities compensates the capitalists as **consumers** but does not alter the tendency to a falling rate of profit.
4. In so far as the cheapening also affects the factors included in constant capital, it counteracts the tendency to a falling rate of profit.
5. "Capital," Vol. I, Chap. 25, pp. 642 et seq.
6. The average figure of unemployment among trade unionists in Germany in the years 1907-1913, that is, in the period which includes the grave crisis of 1907-1908, amounted to 2.3 per cent. Compare with that

1923	1924	1925	1926	1927
9.6	13.5	6.7	18	8.8

—("Statistical Year Book of Germany," p. 536. 1927 calculated by author.)

7. One example from a thousand: Professor Hombert, writing in the "Miners' Journal' of 23-10-27, says: "We must not allow ourselves to be puzzled by the fact that rationalisation as we have seen it has temporarily displaced a large number of workers. That was also the case 100 years ago, when machines entered into competition with human labour power. In the long run, it is true that all technical and economic improvements will indubitably increase the opportunities for labour in any country."
8. Formerly such compensation applied only to imperialist countries: mass unemployment was avoided by the export of industrial products to the colonies, where countless millions

of Indian, Chinese and other hand-workers were displaced and left to die of hunger.

9. "Commerce Year Book," 1926, Vol. 7, p. 16. Figures for building, where there was a great increase in the number of workers employed, are lacking.
10. These figures include the farmers themselves, as well as agricultural labourers; but this does not change the direction of development.
11. Commerce Year Book, 1926, Vol. 1, p. 18.
12. Only first-class railways; hence the difference from the previous table.
13. New index of the Federal Reserve Board, average daily production of the years 1923-4.5 taken as 100.
14. Board of Labour index, 1923-100. "Statistical Abstract," 1926, p. 337.
15. Calculated by the author.
16. "Hochkapitalismus," p. 243.
17. Insured workers from "Labour Gazette": the following are not included in the total: distributive trades, commerce, banking, government, hotels, etc., and also the unemployed.
18. London and Cambridge Economic Service, 1913-100.
19. The large number of workers employed in the years immediately following the war was the result of development during the war and of demobilisation; the decline is therefore not only due to technical improvements and rationalisation, but is to some extent a return to the former "normal" conditions.
20. "Analyst,"9-3-28.
21. Considered in the abstract, this involves a tremendous waste of labour power. As Marx says ("Capital," Vol. 1, p. 540): "From a social point of view, the productiveness increases in the same ratio as the economy of labour, which, in its turn, includes not only economy of the means of production, but also the avoidance of all useless labour. The capitalist mode of production, while on the one hand enforcing economy in each individual business, on the other hand begets by its anarchical system of competition, the most outrageous squandering of labour power and of the social means of production, not to mention the creation of a vast number of employments at present indispensable, but in themselves superfluous."

4

The Sharpening of Contradictions: Rationalisation

"Rationalisation" is a new word for an old phenomenon. Capitalism has always tried, by improvements in technology, by more refined methods of exploitation, to reduce costs of production and so increase profits. But in the last few years this has occurred systematically and at a more rapid rate. To understand these processes we must first of all analyse the various methods of rationalisation according to their economic nature.

In our opinion we must first of all differentiate between three processes:

(*a*) *Raising the profits of an undertaking or of one form of capital at the expense of the profits of other undertakings or forms of capital.* This is a re-division among the capitalists of an unchanged total of surplus value; a process which at the time does not in the least affect the working class. If, for example, a number of undertakings are made into a monopoly, prices raised and profits consequently increased, the effects of this process are confined entirely to the circle of capitalists, if for the time being we make the theoretical assumption that labour power is sold at its proper value; the process does not alter either the rate of exploitation of the workers or the proportions in which the product is divided between the working class and the capitalist class as a whole. Nor does this process affect the amount of labour time embodied in the commodities, or the total sum of products.

This section also includes measures which raise the profits of one form of capital at the expense of other forms. If, for example, industrial capital disposes of its goods directly to the ultimate consumer, thereby eliminating trading capital, then the profits of industrial capital—although the period of turnover is extended—are increased at the expense of trading capital profits. This process also does not affect the value of the product nor the division of the product between capitalists and workers.

(*b*) *The second group of measures of rationalisation includes those processes which involve a decrease in the value of the product.* These are: increasing the productivity of labour; diminishing the labour time embodied in the commodities by standardisation.

An increase in the productivity of labour through technical innovations is the classic form of progress in capitalist production. Each worker sets in motion a more complicated machine, makes with the same expenditure of labour a greater change in the material of his labour, and produces a greater mass of use value than before. We shall deal with technical progress in the last decade in a separate chapter.

As far as standardisation is concerned there is a saving in labour time not through improved technique but through the elimination of those variations in form and size which are superfluous from the point of view of the use value of the commodities, by which, in accordance with the law of mass production, labour time is saved. Commodities satisfying the same demand are produced with the expenditure of less labour time.[1]

To this category belong also measures to avoid waste in raw materials, unnecessary transport, etc.[2] There is nothing new in this. Marx himself dealt with this thoroughly in many places, particularly in the chapter "Economy in the Employment of Constant Capital." But in America it is now being systematically carried out under the patronage of the Government.

(*c*) *The third form of rationalisation is the raising of the rate of surplus value, the increased exploitation of labour power.* We shall now deal with this aspect of rationalisation.

An increase in exploitation can occur by the production of relative surplus value. When, as the result of the methods of rationalisation enumerated above, the prices of goods consumed by the workers fall, the value of labour power falls also, the necessary labour decreases, the surplus labour increases.

An increase in exploitation also follows from a rise in absolute surplus value, either by an extension of hours of labour or by an increase in the intensity of labour. At a certain point the two methods become mutually exclusive; with very great intensity of labour the daily or weekly hours of labour cannot go beyond a certain maximum, or otherwise the worker would break down.

But it is more advantageous to capital to allow a shorter working day with a maximum intensity of labour, than it is to have a longer day with a lower intensity, for constant capital (particularly the fixed part of it) is in this way better employed, because a certain section of expenditure, lighting, heating, administration, supervision, etc. remains the same whether more or less is produced per day.

This explains the tendency of capital to employ a greater amount of labour power in the shortest time. To accomplish this, capitalism has founded a new science, that of scientific management. Piece wages take the place of time rates. The premium system takes the place of simple time rates—that is an increase in piece rates if a certain height of production is reached. And in place of the premium system, or combined with it, the minimum system, every worker who does not reach a certain minimum of production is dismissed. This is combined with time studies, with the dissection of labour into separate, exactly determined and strictly circumscribed movements of the worker.

All this refers to the pre-war period. The latest development shows a dialectical change: *back to time rates, but in conjunction with the introduction of the travelling belt.* The travelling belt in conjunction with "serial" production[3] makes the Taylor system, with all its tremendous supervising and preparatory apparatus, time and movement studies, time cards for each kind of labour and for each worker, entirely superfluous. The travelling belt establishes an automatic control of labour productivity, keeps up the worker to the speed of the travelling belt, enforces a superhuman intensity in the expenditure of labour power. Its employment can be observed in all spheres. Motors and machines move along the travelling belt in just the same way as slaughtered animals in the packing factory, the ingredients in a confectionery works, or the incoming mail at an American sorting station.[4]

The use of travelling belts leads to a multiplication of labour intensity, without raising the productivity of labour. We give a few examples from many:

> "In a Silesian shirt factory the same articles were, in the sewing department, dealt with by different methods of work, resulting in astonishing differences in the length of time required to perform the given task. One method, that formerly used in the department, consisted in the following: each sewer received a certain number of, e.g., men's shirts, and sewed them from the separate parts supplied by the cutter into the finished garment. By the second method, a group of six machines were given a certain amount of work to do, each having to perform a certain part of the work. This involved no change in the arrangement of seats or in technical apparatus. The third method was to employ the idea of the travelling belt: the work was further subdivided and the workers sat in a long row at the appropriate distance from each other. The pieces of work were carried along this row by a simple moving belt, not in an unbroken movement, but regulated so that the belt moved the length

between two workers at intervals of 18 minutes. Within that 18 minutes each worker had to do the required section of work for five shirts. According to the factory management's statistics, which were confirmed by the workers themselves, the following results were given by the three methods in a uniform period of time:

Individual work	100
Group work	260
Travelling belt	350

This result is the more remarkable because, with the exception of the travelling belt itself, no increase or improvement of technical apparatus was necessary. This is a case of an extraordinary improvement in production occasioned by nothing except a better organisation of labour."[5]

This and similar examples show that the *increase in labour output* by rationalisation is only partly due to an increase in the productivity of labour brought about by technical changes, *and to a much greater extent is simply the result of increasing the intensity of labour.* If the monotony of work at the machines is soul destroying—as Engels so powerfully describes it in his *Conditions of the English Working Class*, then work with the travelling belt unmercifully sucks out the strength of the worker to a much greater extent daily than can be renewed.[6] Workers in such conditions are in a state of permanent over-fatigue:

> "With the beginning of this fatigue, the production of the worker remains at the same level—he is not in the least aware of his state of fatigue, nor can it be objectively demonstrated, for the output remains the same.... The gradual increase of the burden of work is not apparent to the worker, because the process works itself out slowly.... Any light illness can then make the state of affairs at once obvious or the worker himself realises in time that 'something has gone wrong'.... The impossibility of recognising the slow appearance of these indefinite results of fatigue is one of the saddest facts which wrecks any attempt at the scientific limitation of admissible labour intensity."[7]

This murderous rate of work has in some cases in America

been still further increased by *the workers having each to work at two travelling bands* (e.g., in the Hudson Essex automobile factory).

This intensity of labour in America, increased to the utmost limit, explains why real wages, in spite of great unemployment, have up to the present shown an upward tendency; why some concerns have introduced the five-day week. The expenditure of labour power enforced by the travelling belt is possible only with good nourishment and a relatively shorter working day, for otherwise, the worker would simply break down at his job. And as cattle are better fed for harder work, capitalism is compelled to give more fodder and grant more resting time than formerly to the human automata working at a pitch of intensity hitherto unknown.[8]

In spite of the rise in real wages, the rate of surplus value in American industry is rising. (There are no statistical data on which to base a calculation for other countries.)

Rate of Surplus Value in American Industry

1914	1919	1921	1923	1925
121	122	106	118	128

The low rate of surplus value in 1921 reflects the crisis. (For the method of calculation see Appendix. The rates of surplus value calculated here are *lower* than is the case actually, for profits of trading capital had to be left out of account.)

Thus we can observe the following line of development as a result of rationalisation, which only accentuates the tendencies inherent in capitalism.

Absolute decrease in the number of workers employed by industrial capital, and, at the same time, an increased growth in the intensity of labour and a rise in the rate of surplus value. This is accompanied by a fall in the average rate of profit as a result of the rapid increase in the organic composition of capital. As a whole there is a strong resemblance to the theoretical picture of pure capitalism painted by Marx—particularly in the United States, the leading capitalist country. There is also a process going on which is establishing two rates of profit. Capital included in monopolies is realising a higher rate of profit at the expense of capital not monopolised and of the independent producers. Because of this, and because of the decrease in the total wages of the working class as a result of rationalisation, there is a narrowing down of the home market and, in spite of monopolies, a more acute struggle for markets which must necessarily lead to war and to a further redivision of the world....

NOTES

1. The following figures concerning the United States show what great success has in many cases been obtained in reducing variety in the same article of use:

	Reduction of types		
	from	*to*	*per cent*
Glazed tiles	66	4	94
Beds	78	4	95
Ordinary tiles	44	1	98
Kettles	130	13	90
Forged tools	665	351	47
Milk bottles	78	10	87
Iron plates	1,819	263	85
Warehouse slips	1,000	15	850

(Dr. Bruno Birnbaum: "Organisation of Rationalisation: America-Germany." Berlin, 1927.)

Tugwell gives other interesting examples in his above-mentioned book, p. 136. A felt hat factory produced 3,684 kinds of hats. He remarks that 90 per cent of its sales occurred in seven kinds of hats in 10 shades. Production was therefore confined to those varieties. A shoe factory turned out 2,500 kinds of shoes in three qualities. This was reduced to 100 kinds of one quality. By this means costs of production were lowered by 30 per cent, general factory costs by 28 per cent, and sale price by 27 per cent. Sales rose by 50 per cent.

2. The struggle against waste is one of the principal objects of American economic policy. See, e.g. Stuart Chase, "The Tragedy of Waste," New York, 1926.
3. The new organisation of labour "... is concerned with two essential factors of productive labour: machine and human activity in a new manner: with mass production, ... the processes of labour are dealt with not, as in most former instances of 'serial' production, **next to each other,** but **after each other.** While with 'serial' production the piece of work, so to speak, goes in search of the appropriate machine, with 'travelling' work the continuous stream of work determines where the required machine is to stand. There is no more turning, cutting, planing, but the lathes, cutting machines and planing machines stand between drilling machines, polishing machines, casting machines, in positions necessitated by the time taken by the travelling labour process." (Dr. L. Preller in "National Labour Journal," 1927, No. 5. Quoted in "Rote Fahne," 26-4-28.)
4. See J. Hirsch: "The American Economic Miracle."
5. Tarnov: "Why be Poor?" p. 31.
6. Sombart has pertinently stated the motto for the modern factory worker:
   "The soul must be left in the cloakroom on entry."
   "Though operations have becomes specialised, skill has become less so, and in large stretches of industry labour has become merely automatic machine-tending. In short, American labour today is, to a degree little realised, unskilled labour—the standardisation imposed upon the product has also been stamped upon the man." ("Times," 9-3-28.)
7. Prof. Arnold During: "National Labour Journal," 1928, No. 2.
8. "...where we have labour, not carried on by fits and starts, but repeated day after day with unvarying uniformity, a point must inevitably be reached where extension of the working day and intensity of labour naturally exclude one another, in such a way that lengthening of the working day becomes compatible only with a lower degree of intensity, and a higher degree of intensity only with a shortening of the working day." ("Capital," Vol. I, p. 400.)

5

The New Technique and Its Economic Consequences

> With the single exception of the era which saw the introduction of steam, probably none has witnessed a greater industrial revolution than that in progress today. Changes are taking place in every direction, and many of the conditions under which the great staple industries were built up no longer exist. Electrical energy, generated in many countries by water power hitherto running to waste, has vastly extended the area in which manufacturing can be successfully conducted; it is no longer anchored to accessible coal. Chemical discoveries...have altered the relative values of raw materials. The development of many new countries, which has been largely due to modern means of communication, has led to a great change in the relative importance of the world's markets. In the midst of this changing world new industries, not only in this country, have come into being to meet new requirements..." ("The Times," 17-3-28.)

In the last few years there has been a rapid increase in the output of labour. This is based upon an increased intensity and productivity of labour.[1] Increased productivity is a result of numerous technical innovations which have recently been introduced in connection with rationalisaiton.[2] It is not our concern to deal with the purely technical aspect of the question, nor have we the technical knowledge for such a task. We can only try to infer the economic consequences of technical development.

THE ECONOMICS OF POWER

We shall begin with power. The following processes must be distinguished.

(*a*) The better employment of coal,[3] steam turbines in place of the old steam engines,[4] flexible furnaces, coal dust fuel, the beginning of long-distance gas conducting, and liquefaction of coal.

(*b*) Replacement of coal by oil, peat, water power.

Economic result, international coal crisis!

In spite of progressing industrialisation and the great increase in the volume of production there is no increase in the amount of coal being used. This is most clearly shown in the United States. Production, which we may take as indicative of consumption, amounted to

Production, million tons (5 yearly averages)[5]

	1870	*1880*	*1890*	*1900*	*1910*	*1920*	*1925*	*1927*
	32	62	13	227	455	626	559	601
Percentage increase	—	94	123	65	200	38	–11	7

Following on a serious decline in the upward trend for the periods 1905-10 and 1915-20, there is an absolute decrease in consumption.

(*c*) *Steam engines are no longer employed as machines for labour*, as in Marx's time, *but for the generation of electrical power.* As steam power was important in the age of free capitalist competition, so electrical power is important for the age of imperialism. And instead of small electrical concerns satisfying local requirements we now have gigantic works engaged in generating electricity on the site of the actual source of energy (waterfalls and coal mines) and high-tension transmission across very great distances.[6]

The economic consequences of the change to electrical high-tension power are as follows:

(1) *Greater freedom for industry to choose its site of production: the decentralisation of large-scale industry*. The direct use of steam power compelled many industries to set up works on a site as near as possible to the coal areas or in their immediate vicinity, otherwise the freightage costs of coal would have increased the costs of production.[7] By covering the whole country with a high-tension network, industry can move either to the area of raw materials or to the localities where cheap labour is obtainable. We can observe a great moving of industry in the U.S.A. from the north-east to the south, in England from the north to the south-east. Industry, formerly concentrated preponderantly in the neighbourhood of coal, is being distributed: the economic structure of the different industrial countries is being equalised, the division into purely agricultural areas and mainly industrial areas is being eliminated. The industrial proletariat, as a class, is spread over the whole country!

(2) The use of electrical high-tension transmission affords a concrete basis for the rapid development of certain areas whose economic development in the age of steam power was hindered by lack of coal. The rapid development of north Italian industry in the last decade would have been impossible without the transmission of electrical energy from the Alps. Long-distance high-tension transmission makes it possible to exploit industrially those areas which produce raw materials and which are badly developed in the way of communications. (Important for Africa and Asia.)[8]

(3) *The concentration of power supply*. The technical development of electricity generation enforces the interconnection of electricity power stations in a country, the object being to even out the variations in daily and seasonal consumption. Over large areas in Germany and the United States generating stations are connected up with each other (small works are mostly closed down and production concentrated in a small number of large stations).[9] The central electrical power stations have become decisive economic rulers.[10]

The cessation of electric power supply caused by a general strike with a revolutionary mass movement would have much more decisive effects in the great industrial countries than a strike in any other branch of industry.

(4) *Greater mobility within the factory.* Factories working directly on steam power, as Marx described them, were concerns working in a unified manner.

> "An organised system of machines, to which motion is communicated by the transmitting mechanism from a central automation, is the most developed form of production by machinery. Here we have, in the place of the isolated machine, a mechanical monster whose body fills whole factories, and whose demon power, at first veiled under the slow and measured motions of his giant limbs, at length breaks out into the fast and furious whirl of his countless working organs."[11]

The replacement of steam power by electricity has changed the appearance of factories.[12] The "unified impulse" of the steam engine disappears. "The transmitting mechanism, composed of flywheels, shafting, toothed wheels, pulleys, straps, ropes, bands, pinions and gearing of the most varied kinds"[13] is almost completely disappearing. The factory as a whole is absolutely dependent upon the supply of electricity, but—that guaranteed—is more mobile and elastic than the old steam factory. Indeed, the idea of complete decentralisation of the factory, of the re-emergence of rural industry on a modern basis, has arisen.[14]

PROGRESS IN MACHINERY ITSELF

It is difficult to characterise this generally, because it consists of innumerable details. Although certain special new machines greatly assisting production have been introduced (e.g. the Westlake bottle machine) there has not been, as far as we can see, any fundamental, revolutionary change in any branch of industry which works up its raw materials by machinery. Innovations have proceeded in the old channels:

further division of the processes of labour and multiplication of special machines for dealing with detailed jobs,[15] mechanisation of the transport of raw materials to the machine, making the labour processes automatic, etc. This last factor has been of great importance, particularly in the textile industry. Human labour is limited entirely to supervision. In America one worker and two assistants tend 60 machines. We are of the opinion that the increase in labour output is due less to improvements in machinery than to improvements in the organisation of labour. The greatest increase has been in the intensity of labour, and only secondarily in productivity.

The development of agricultural machinery is in a rather exceptional position. In this case the universal machine and not the specialised machine is the object aimed at; a natural consequence of the fact that a certain process has to be carried out only once a year and then for a short period. Hence the development of all-round agricultural machines, moved by tractors, in which the actual implements are interchangeable at will, e.g. one machine for harvesting and threshing.[16] The economic consequences are : a great increase in the organic composition of capital in agriculture, decreased opportunity for work on the land, and a change in unemployment from being "latent" into being acute.

The employment of machinery in offices also occupies a peculiar position. It decreases the overhead coals of the capitalist system of production by systematising the keeping of accounts, and by replacing clerks, statisticians and book-keepers by machines tended largely by unskilled workers. The machine, which groups thousands of items on cards in the form of punched holes, adds and gives the complete calculation; the "human machine," a recent American invention which deals with accounts transmitted by telephone, indicates the line of development. A similar change is taking place in the rearrangement of labour, e.g. clocking in on separate cards, instead of in books; the conveyor carrying book-keeping documents from one employee to the other. The economic consequence is a relative surplus of office workers who—as in agriculture and industry—presently become an absolute surplus.

THE CONVEYOR AS THE CENTRE OR ORGANISATION

The important changes have not taken place in machinery but in the organisation of labour within the factories. The real centre of the factory is not in the machine, but in the travelling belt. It is not the materials of labour which, on their way through the factory, are adapted to the machinery, it is not the materials of labour which journey from machine to machine, as formerly, but the other way round. The organisational centre is the conveyor, and the machines are so placed as to serve the requirements of conveyor work. The most varied machines are placed along the conveyor in gay confusion; the necessary tools for the workers, if they have to change their tools at all, are placed ready to hand. The old factory organisation, the coordination of similar machines or machine systems, is disappearing.

The essential condition for the successful employment of the travelling belt is mass production, the production of exactly similar commodities in unbroken repetition. With the products of the great staple industries, cotton yarn and fabrics, metals, etc., this has been the case for some time. What is new is the extension of mass production to the means of production or their parts (standardisation), and also to articles of consumption (automobiles, houses, shoes, clothes).

The essential condition for mass production is a large market for the commodities produced. This arises partly from the standardisation of demand[17]—which has proceeded furthest in America—and partly from a general increase in the sale of the particular commodity.[18]

Production with the conveyor requires not only a large

market, but a correspondingly great capital; it promotes concentration and centralisation and the formation of monopolies.

The economic nature of production with the conveyor is the attainment of the greatest possible output. The arrangement of labour within the factory also serves this purpose: the elimination of any superfluous movement from the labour process on the one hand, and the production of the greatest intensity of labour on the other.[19] The speed of work has been so greatly accelerated that in many concerns compulsory rest intervals had to be introduced, for otherwise some of the workers would certainly have broken down during the day....

THE ADVANCE OF THE CHEMICAL INDUSTRY

Tremendous progress has been made in the chemical industry. Together with electrification the chemical industry gives the technology of today its peculiar character. The production of nitrogen from the air, liquefaction of coal, artificial silk, regeneration of used rubber, synthetic rubber, etc.

The age of capitalism was distinguished from pre-capitalist epochs, as Sombart has correctly remarked, by substituting inorganic for organic materials; substituting the products of mining for those of agriculture and forestry—iron instead of wood for tools and materials of construction, coal instead of wood for fuel, petroleum instead of vegetable matter for lighting, etc. Development today is along the lines of replacing rare by "ubiquitous"—the word is Weber's—raw materials, that is, by raw materials which are found everywhere. Iron and wood are to be replaced by concrete, saltpetre by nitrogen, natural petroleum by liquefied coal, silk by artificial silk, etc.

This development also implies the replacement of mechanical by chemical labour. Instead of coal being transported in its natural condition it will be turned into electrical energy, gas or oil, and conducted great distances by wires or pipes without any mechanical labour.[20] Instead of felling and sawing wood, instead of digging for iron ore, smelting and rolling iron, cement will be produced. Electrolysis is gaining a growing importance in metallurgy; quite new metals (e.g. aluminium for aeroplanes) are obtaining economic importance.

Economically, this implies a tendency towards the distribution of industry over the whole country, instead of its former concentration in areas producing either fuel or raw materials, with the results which we mentioned above.

The advance in chemistry at the expense of the mechanical working up of raw materials also implies an advance in apparatus at the expense of machinery in the whole system of capitalist production.

> "The machine proper is therefore a mechanism that, after being set in motion, performs with its tools the same operations that were formerly done by the workman with similar tools." (*Capital*, I, p. 368.)

This definition of the machine is not applicable to the mechanism of production in chemical industry. The means of production in the chemical industry are not machines, but apparatus, appropriately constructed container-and-pipe systems in which the objects of labour are handled, and machine processes, such as mixing, shaking and turning, play only an accessory part.[21] Production is becoming automatic; most businesses are almost entirely empty of workers!

Apparatus production implies a sharp division of labour power in the works concerned, there are no skilled apparatus workers. In the chemical industry there are chemical engineers, about one-fifth of the total personnel; the rest are unskilled workers who do the work of assistants, understand nothing of the processes of production and on the whole are very badly paid.[22]

PROGRESS IN TRAFFIC

In the nineteenth century railways were the most important factor in overcoming crises and in the opening of new areas for the capitalist mode of production, as Lenin demonstrated in his *Imperialism*. The war and the post-war period showed a relative slowing down in railway construction.[23] In shipbuilding the former development was continued; in the place of the steam-ship came the motor-ship, in the place of coal firing came oil as fuel. New sailing vessels for long-distance voyages were no longer built; the attempt to utilise wind in shipping in a new form, *Flettner's Rotor Ship*, does not seem to be gaining any economic importance. In recent shipbuilding the greatest importance is attached to speed and comfortable, elegant arrangements for passengers. Automobiles and aeroplanes are gaining the lead. The figures are generally known; we shall only refer to the economic consequences.

The automobile makes it possible to link up to the world transport system those thinly-populated areas where railways, on account of the little traffic, would not pay. There are motor roads from the Mediterranean to Bagdad right through Arabia, there is Trans-Sahara transport, etc.

Automobile and air transport establish a very rapid connection between all quarters of the globe. Development is proceeding rapidly. Ford is beginning to manufacture cheap mass aeroplanes, the flight over the Atlantic Ocean has been accomplished,[24] there are motors without fuel,[25] rocket automobiles and aeroplanes.[26]

Motor and air transport serve chiefly to shorten the time of journeys for travellers. The motor mainly for shorter distances, for connecting up the main railway lines and also town and country. It enables those employed in the town at fairly well-paid jobs to live in the country. It is also rapidly becoming of great importance in freight traffic for short distances, and is successfully entering into competition with the railways for short distances.[27]

Aeroplanes have up to the present only been used in exceptional circumstances for transporting very expensive commodities, for which long delay in transport would involve great loss of interest, or for articles which spoil quickly. This applies to the transport of gold from England to the Continent, and in South Africa; of fresh flowers and fruit from the South of France to London, etc. Its greater importance is for passenger traffic over long distances, particularly if there is no good overland route. In these cases the saving in time is very great indeed. The pressure towards saving time gave rise to the many attempts to cross the Atlantic Ocean by air; it can scarcely be doubted that within a few years there will be a regular air transport service between America and Europe.

The contradiction between the development of transport technique and the division of the capitalist world into numerous small States is becoming more and more acute. Frontier crossing and tariff formalities will soon occupy more time than the journeys themselves.

PROGRESS IN THE DISTRIBUTION OF INFORMATION

The last decade has witnessed great progress in the technique of distributing information. Postal transmission by means of motors and aeroplanes has resulted in great rapidity in spreading information. The most important innovation, however, is that contained in the radio, the wireless transmission of news. Radio connects the most distant areas with the centre, and since it requires no cables, the number of those using it can be illimitably extended. The one-sidedness arising from the fact that one can only receive news, but that only the distributing centre can send out news, will soon be overcome. The radio telephone and radio-vision are about to be put into operation.[28] Trans-oceanic cables, for whose possession the imperialists fought so bitterly ten years ago at the conclusion of peace, will soon be worthless rubbish....

Progress in the technique of transport and news distribution has greatly improved knowledge of the world market. Differences in prices arising from a lack of knowledge of market conditions in distant areas, and the speculation which took place because of this, have disappeared. So has the possibility of carrying on credit swindles, which, even in Marx's time, greatly intensified crises.[29] Connections in world economy are growing closer; and the possibilities of crises arising from ignorance of what is happening, less. Crises are now much more due to inherent causes, and much less to accidents.

TECHNOLOGY AND MILITARY PREPARATIONS

The reason for employing technical inventions is found in the desire of capitalist undertakings to increase their profits. It would, however, be false to overlook the close connection between technique and war preparations, to ignore the fact that many technical inventions were made in the course of the war, and have been put into operation in the hope of making large profits in the next war, meanwhile being supported by the Government. The production of nitrogen from the air originated in Germany during the war, because the supply of saltpetre was cut off; the same is true of the English and American dyestuffs industry, because of the lack of German dyes. The entire chemical industry is most closely connected with war preparations, and this is also true of transport. Civil aviation in all capitalist countries is subsidised by the Government. The British Empire Lines have never yet covered their expenses by their own income. But governments everywhere subsidise civil aviation, for in case of war, every aeroplane will immediately be used for military service; every civil pilot is a potential military pilot. Every technical innovation is immediately tested to see what use could be made of it in a future war.[30] The great industrial countries are gaining an absolute military predominance over the agricultural and smaller countries which, as a result of their incapacity to equip themselves from a technical and military standpoint out of their own resources, can only take part in war as a part of one of the alliances led by an industrial Great Power.

TECHNOLOGY AND ECONOMICS

We shall now try to recapitulate the economic consequences of the new technique, with all the reservations which are unavoidable in a subject with which we are so little familiar.[31] *The most widespread result is that the contradictions in capitalism have been intensified*!

(*a*) The new technique and organisation of labour has increased output to such an extent that the "setting free" of workers is no longer compensated for by an extension in the domain of the capitalist system of production. While Marx witnessed an increase in the number of workers despite technical progress, today we are faced with unemployment on a gigantic scale, with an increasing army of permanently unemployed in the most highly developed capitalist countries. A diminished number of productive workers are working with a murderous intensity, while millions are unemployed!

(*b*) The contradiction between production capacity and the possibilities of realisation is growing sharper. The decrease in variable capital, i.e. in the share of total product falling to the working class, means the narrowing down of the home market and gives rise to the necessity for a more bitter conflict for markets outside the "national" market. Simultaneously, a considerable part of the machinery of production is lying idle!

(*c*) The rapid technical development increases the danger of "moral waste," of machinery becoming prematurely out-of-date. This explains the tendency towards the greatest possible utilisation of stock, although this is hindered by the narrowness of the market.

(*d*) The organic composition of capital is increasing rapidly. This enforces the concentration of capital, for it requires a huge amount of capital to start a new concern capable of competing. Hence the tendency towards the formation of monopolies.

(*e*) The contradiction between social production and private ownership in the means of production is growing stronger; technical development makes the concentration of capital a necessity. This tendency can be seen partly expressed in State capitalism.

(*f*) The latest technique liberates industry from being bound to particular areas, enables previously backward areas to develop rapidly, diminishes the contrast between town and country, increases the connections of all quarters of the globe with world economy.

(*g*) As against this, the latest technique adds to the economic, military and political predominance of the great imperialist industrial countries. The resistance of the smaller countries, expressed in high protective tariffs, gives rise to the break-up of the world market, without affecting the superiority of the great industrial countries.

In the following chapters we shall deal with some of these factors more fully.

NOTES

1. Since these two ideas are often confused, we shall differentiate exactly between them: **By productivity of labour we understand that factor in labour output which is determined by the means of production.** With the same expenditure of labour power for the same period of time, the output can be greater or less according to the nature and quality of the means of production employed. The use of better machinery, better technique, raises the productivity of labour. **The intensity of labour is determined by the quantity of labour power expended in a given period of time**. (In the words of Marx,

"The expenditure of human muscular energy, blood, nerves.") It is the number of appropriate movements, of necessary muscular energy, the degree of nerve strain, etc. A change in the intensity of labour can take place while using the same machinery, according to the rate at which it is worked. Increases in the productivity and intensity of labour generally occur simultaneously, but this is not necessarily so. There can be increased intensity with unchanged productivity, but scarcely the reverse. Increased productivity of labour means the production of a greater quantity of consumable values with the same expenditure of human labour power, that is, decreasing value per unit of product. Increased intensity similarly means the production of a greater quantity of consumable values, but in this case their value is proportionately greater, because more intensive labour in the same time is as creative of value as labour of normal intensity employed for a longer time. (See "Capital," Vol. III, Section 2.)

2. We must differentiate sharply between the discovery and introduction of new machines. Often years and decades pass before a new technical invention is sufficiently widespread to effect a change in production; and only in the latter case has it economic importance.
3. Considering coal from the beginning in the mine up to its utilisation as fuel in a steam engine, only 4 per cent of its power was usefully employed because of waste and faulty technique. (American Geological Survey and the Bureau of Mines. Quoted, "Waste in Industry," p. 241.)
4. The great progress made in the use of coal in recent years is shown by numerous data. According to the management of the Austrian Federal Railways, the following amounts of coal were employed per 1,000 British ton miles:

1923	1924	1925	1926	1927
157	126	113	107	104

("Exchange Courier," 20-12-27)

5. Stat. Abstract of U.S.A. 1926, p. 725. Percentages calculated by the author.
6. Electricity generated in the Alps is conducted to towns in Lombardy. Electricity up to a pressure of 100,000 volts is transmitted hundreds of miles in America.
7. See Weber's excellent book: "The Site of Industry," Tubingen,

1907.

8. The importance of electrical power will become still greater should Marconi's attempt to transmit power by radio succeed, for cables are very expensive.
9. This development in America has been summed up in two phrases, "super-power" and "giant power." The name of super-power is given to the system by which the individual electric supply companies retain their independence, their connection with each other only consisting of the distribution of their surplus power among themselves. Giant power means the concentration of the total production of, and the total demand for, electricity in a whole State, and correspondingly systematic distribution. (See "Giant Power," special number, "Annals of American Academy for Social Sciences," March, 1925.)
10. The formation of giant power under private ownership "would be the most dangerous monopoly that has yet existed."—Pinchot, Governor of Pennsylvania, in the special number of the "Annals."
11. "Capital," Vol. I, p. 377.
12. In the U.S.A. 75 per cent, and in Germany about 50 per cent of all factories work with electric power.
13. "Capital," Vol. I, p. 367.
14. Irwin Fisher in "Giant Power."
15. The shoe industry is a good example of this. See E.J. Jones, "The Trust Problem in the U.S.A."
16. Julius Hirsch, in the "Berliner Tageblatt" for 28-2-28, makes a few interesting observations on the growing importance of machines in American agriculture. The following are the number of horses in the United States:

1915	21,200,000
1920	19,900,000
1925	16,500,000
1927	15,300,000
1932 (estimated)	12,000,000

The estimate for 1932 is based on the present number of foals. Of the most recent machines adopted in American agriculture the following are worthy of attention: (1) The so-called "Little Combine," which is a combination of moving, binding and threshing machine. The employment of these machines is, of course, only possible in dry areas, where the corn can be cut quite dry. Such a machine costs 1,285 dollars. The department calculated that the employment of such a machine effected a saving of about 21s. per ton. Recently they are coming to be used in their tens of thousands. (2) The tractor has also been greatly improved, so that it can now be used both for small plots of ground and for hilly, stony and boggy soil. A main-wheel tractor, strong enough for ploughing, is now being sold at 750 dollars, and also, of course, on the hire-purchase system. There is also the mechanical cotton picker. This is still in an experimental stage, and has the disadvantage of leaving more than a quarter of the crop untouched. But doubtless this will be remedied.

17. While there did exist formerly a conventional similarity in the clothing, houses, etc., of the workers engaged in domestic industry or in handicrafts, serial production today enforces a new uniformity of demand. In America millions own the same Ford car, the same shoes, the same bookcases with the same 50 or 100 "best books," etc.

18. The lack of sufficient markets is the chief danger which confronts German rationalisation. The whole tragedy of German rationalisation was aptly described by a German correspondent of the "Statist" in the issue of 10-3-28 in the following words:

    "The world's excessive demand for German products... gave place to an almost complete lack of orders from abroad after the stabilisation of the mark. German goods seemed to have lost suddenly the ability to compete in external markets, whereas German imports of foreign, chiefly American, articles rose steadily. Their lower price, notwithstanding the far higher earnings of labourers in the United States, led in 1925 to a migration of the captains of trade and industry across the ocean in order to see for themselves how America could succeed in underbidding German industry even in its home market....Upon the return of these explorers 'The rationalisation of production methods' became the catchword in Germany. It was said that merely by imitating the American practice of recklessly scrapping out-of-date machinery and of mass production of certain standard types, the growing adversity of the German trade balance could be checked and the foreign demand for German articles could be re-established. But... the goal of rationalisation was not reached... and the market for German goods abroad showed no increase... The only positive results of the rationalisation process appear to be an over-expansion of the production capacity of German industry and an immense increase of its indebtedness, particularly to foreign countries. Responsible for this failure is the blind imitation of American methods. No attention has been paid to the fact that the United States industry has a far wider domestic market than Germany, and does not beat itself against insurmountable Customs barriers in the immediate vicinity of its headquarters."

19. The importance of the organisation of labour as compared with developments in machinery is shown by the following:

    According to the Balfour Report (Part II.–Further Factors in Industrial Efficiency, p.11) the increase in wage-costs per unit of product between 1907 and 1924 was greater than the increase in a full week's wages (with the exception of heavy industry, shipbuilding and machine construction). Also the mechanical power employed in industry rose much more than production per head (from 8,000,000 to 13,500,000 h.p.). The reasons for this were, insufficient employment of labour power, widespread short time, high overhead charges. Since 1924 the position has improved as a result of the rationalisation then begun.

20. In England and Germany about half the transport of goods is done by coal; this explains the opposition of the railways to long-distance conveying of gas. The necessary condition for long-distance gas conveying is the invention of welded steel pipes which will stand a pressure of 30 atmospheres; a riveted pipe as used formerly, will not stand such a pressure.

21. There appeared before the war a Marxist book on this problem, to which too little attention has been paid, which is even more topical today, "Machines, Tools and Apparatus," by Mataré.

22. The technique of the chemical industry, which has always been kept a secret, is rapidly changing. The principal chemists of the International Dyestuffs Corporation when they vacate their positions receive their full salaries for three years, but may not accept positions in any other chemical concern. I once

asked a director of that concern, "And if he should go to England or America after the three years?" receiving the answer, "In three years our technique has changed so greatly that he may peacefully enter into competition with us; he can't harm us any longer."

23. The total length of railways in the world amounted to

End of 1913	End of 1924	Increase
1,101,653 km.	1,221,066 km.	11 per cent

("German Statistical Year Book," p. 71.)

24. The Domier works are now turning out giant aeroplanes with 12 motors, totalling 5,000 h.p., for American transport. They are to be equipped with nautical instruments and everything necessary for ocean transport.
25. Early in 1928 in America, Lindbergh, a representative of the War Ministry, the inventor and the capitalist who were backing the invention, tried out a motor which works without fuel, but utilises the electric currents in the earth by means of a magnetic motor. The motor developed 1,800 revolutions per minute, and may be the herald of a revolution in the sphere of transport technology.
26. The rocket automobile was first used in Berlin in May, 1928, and with success. It is claimed that the rocket aeroplane has the advantage of not needing much air for the lifting planes, and can therefore go far from the earth's surface and attain terrific speed. A thousand, even thousands, of kilometres per hour is mentioned.
27. Many complaints about this have been made in England, where the railways are now beginning to organise their own motor transport.
28. Judicial super-structure lags behind economic development here also. Recently in America the courts decided that a cheque transmitted by radio cannot be recognised as valid.
29. See "Capital," Vol. III, : "Credit and Fictitious Capital."
30. The American Brown Boveri Company, in conjunction with a large shipbuilding firm, early in 1928 requested the assistance of the American Government in constructing six 35,000-ton trans-Atlantic passenger steamers. They are to take four days in crossing the Atlantic from dock to dock, and to be equipped as aeroplane carriers. In the plans it was mentioned that the decisions of the Naval Armaments Conference of 1922 do not

refer to these ships, and that no naval Power in the world possesses, or is in process of building, such ships. They are to travel at 33 knots, and can cover more than 7,000 nautical miles without stopping for fuel; and, although their normal equipment would consist of 24 aeroplanes for civil purposes, they can be easily adapted to carry 100 aeroplanes in the event of national need. It is further emphasised that the peculiar advantage of these ships is that they require no travel base, this being of particular importance since the U.S.A. has no marine base west of Hawaii. Government assistance was nominally refused.

31. Some of what is here written has already been commented upon by Comrade Brand at the Seventh Plenum of the Comintern.

6

The Limitation of the Home Market and the Struggle for the World Market

The capitalist system of production has the tendency to decrease the workers' share in the social product, for, with an increase in productivity, those goods which are consumed by the workers fall in value, and necessary labour time becomes shorter, and surplus labour longer. The share of the worker grows less in a corresponding degree. Formerly the share of the working class as a whole, that is, variable capital, only decreased relatively in the great industrial countries. But in the most recent developments there has been an absolute decrease.

We have already referred to the decrease in the number of productive workers in the United States. A smaller number of workers are being exploited at a much greater intensity. More intensive labour requires better nourishment. Hence a slight increase in the real wages of full-time workers. The American Bureau of Labour statistics publishes the following index numbers, based upon returns from more than 10,000 concerns employing more than 3,000,000 workers.[1]

	1923	*1924*	*1925*	*1926*
Number of workers	100.0	90.3	91.2	91.9
Total wages bill	100.0	90.6	93.6	95.8
Cost of living index (1913-100)	173.2	172.5	177.9	175.6

The number of workers has decreased by 8 per cent, the wages bill by 4 per cent. Wages have therefore risen relatively by 4 per cent. But this increase is practically cancelled out by an increase in the cost of living of 2½ per cent. These figures may be taken as typical. For 1926 was a year of good markets.

As for the absolute amounts paid out in wages, we have only the figures for industry as they appear in the census returns.

In Million Dollars[2]

	Wages bill	*Salaries*	*Value added*
1923	10,999	3,001	34,481
1925	10,730	3,147	35,936

Wages down by 270,000,000 dollars, surplus value increased by 1,455,000,000 dollars.

In 1925 industrial workers could buy 270,00,000 dollars worth less of their own products than in 1923, although they had increased the values produced by them by 1,455,000,000 dollars. The same is true of most other branches of production in America (particularly agriculture) as well as of other industrial countries for which there are no figures. This explains the diminishing purchasing capacity of the working class.

The prices of goods produced by monopoly organisations are not lowered in a corresponding degree to the decrease in their cost of production. Monopolist capital gets extra profits beyond the average rate of profit. This is at the expense of the profits of independent producers and unorganised capitalists, farmers, handicraftsmen, petty capitalists, whose purchasing power is proportionately diminished. This involves a further narrowing of the home market. A particular kind of limitation of the home market occurred in the inflation countries, where the income of the rentier classes was expropriated. The consequences of inflation as they affected the home market could not be wiped out for many years.

It may be argued, as has been done by the bourgeois apostles of harmony, that the less the workers, independent producers and unorganised capitalists produce, the more falls to the share of the monopolists; the total purchasing power of society remains the same, the total annual product. Hence the sale of commodities is guaranteed.

This would be so in the case of a regulated economically-planned capitalism, in which production was systematically adapted to the distribution of income. But capitalism today is—in spite of State capitalism and monopolies—an antagonistic and anarchic mode of production, in which each undertaking is anxious to reduce costs of production, for which purpose methods must be employed which must necessarily result in an increase in the volume of production beyond the limits imposed by the antagonistic distribution of income.

This means, first of all, periodically recurring crises, and, secondly, a bitter struggle for foreign markets. This explains one policy, represented chiefly by the reformists: the capitalists should, in their own interests, pay higher wages.[3] The second looks forward to increased consumption on the part of the capitalists themselves. It is true that at the present time the capitalist class is displaying unprecedented luxury, particularly in America. But the Europeans are not behindhand in this, as is shown by the following description of the journey of Loewenstein, the Belgian capitalist, to America. (*New York Times*, 26-3-28.)

> "Mr. Loewenstein is travelling rather in the manner of a ruler than as a private citizen. He is accompanied by his wife and five guests: the Count and Countess de Gurnes, Count and Countess Montalenbert, Commander Daufresne and a personal staff of 15 persons, consisting of four secretaries, two typists, a private detective, a chauffeur, a private pilot, a masseur and a valet. He brought with him on the boat two wonderful automobiles... He will buy a Fokker plane here, which he will use during his stay. The company occupied eight suites and cabins on board... The banker and his wife occupied the most

> luxurious suite, consisting of three bedrooms with baths, a private consulting-room and a private dining-room... The cost of the journey alone amounted to about 20,000 dollars, and a sum of about 3,000 dollars was spent on wireless telegrams sent by Mr. Loewenstein during the journey..."

But so long as there is no economically planned and regulated capitalism— and such there can never be—it is impossible for the capitalists to spend the whole surplus value and give up accumulation.

The struggle for markets is conducted by many methods, such as: (1) industrial high protective tariffs, (2) dumping, (3) capital export, (4) colonial policy.

All countries have *industrial protective tariffs*, Spain and the United States the highest.[4] In England only a few industries are protected by tariffs, but their number is increasing from year to year. In spite of the famous Bankers' Manifesto, in spite of the fine decisions of the World Economic Conference, new commodities are continually being protected with tariffs, and the already existing tariffs raised. The competition between the different national bourgeoisies for markets prevents any reduction in tariffs. The formula corresponding to the interests of the bourgeoisie would be: prohibitively high protective tariffs for ourselves, free trade for all other countries. Since they cannot compel the bourgeoisie of other countries to adopt free trade, they all raise tariff barriers and engage in dumping.

By dumping we mean selling on the foreign market at lower prices than on the home market, in many cases lower even than the actual cost of production. The foreign market is of great importance for national monopolies, for high prices can be maintained at home only so long as no more goods are placed on the market than can be disposed of at such high prices. That is why it is the strongest monopolies which carry on dumping.

Protective tariffs and dumping are contradictory processes: they mutually neutralise each other's effects.

Dumping leads to the establishment of still higher protective tariffs or to international alliances of the national monopoly organisations for the purpose of reserving the home market (the European Steel Cartel).

The export of capital is the principal method employed in the struggle for sales on the world market. The importance of capital export to monopolistic capital was thoroughly analysed by Lenin in *Imperialism*. There is little new to be added to his remarks:

> "In the old type of capitalism, that of free competition, the export of *goods* was the most typical feature. In the modern kind, the capitalism of monopolies, the export of *capital* becomes the typical feature." (*Imperialism,* Chap. IV. p. 69.)

Two factors can be distinguished in capital export, the export of capital for the purpose of exporting goods. This is accomplished in the form of long-term credits, by which the disposition of the goods exported is transferred to the buyer (e.g. the sale of military equipment to foreign States by means of long-term credits).

Capital export proper: capital which, because of the lack of markets and the low rate of profit cannot be invested at a sufficiently profitable rate at home, is invested abroad, in which case the exporters of capital retain control of it (e.g. railway construction and concerns in foreign countries).[5]

These two kinds of capital export are contradictory to each other. Capital export proper creates a market for goods once, but as soon as production is begun abroad, the export of the country of those goods which are produced abroad as a result of capital investment, decreases to a corresponding extent. In spite of this capital export proper is continuing to a great degree, urged on by the high rate of profit in the backward countries.

> "In these backward countries, the profits are generally higher, for capital is scarce, the price of land is relatively small, wages are low, raw materials are cheap. The possibility of the export of capital is created by the entry of numerous backward

> countries into international capitalist life: the most important railway lines are either built or being built there, the elementary conditions for industrial development are in existence, etc." (*Imperialism,* p. 70.)

Before the war western Europe was the only capital-exporting area. But since then the position has changed. The United States has become the greatest capital-exporting country; France is no longer in the ranks of capital-exporting countries, while Germany has become one of the greatest importers of capital.[6] This is a result of the reparation obligations, and will cease when these have been again regulated and the temporary demand for making up the deficiencies caused by inflation and for carrying out rationalisation have been covered.

The best means of ensuring a proportionate share in the world market for the sale of commodities and for capital export, is the acquisition of areas controlled by monopoly, the acquisition of colonies. Hence the urge of the capitalist Powers towards gaining the greatest number of colonies even in the period of free competition. Today this way is no longer open. The earth is already distributed among the imperialist Powers. There still remain South America, but that is under requisition by the United States, Turkey, Persia, Afghanistan, which have, however, freed themselves from the imperialist Powers or are in process of so doing. One large area remains, and it is around this that the struggle is now being waged: *China*.

But, influenced by the existence of the Soviet Union, and by that of the successful opposition offered to the imperialists by Turkey and Afghanistan with its assistance, it requires increasingly great efforts and expenditure to maintain the suppression of the colonial peoples. Moreover, super-profits have been cut down by the working-class movement in the colonies. A larger area has to be controlled in order to obtain the same amount of profit. This explains the sharpening struggle for colonies, for a redivision of the world.

This re-division is openly demanded by the capitalists of those countries whose internal economic development is in contrast to their lack or insufficient ownership of colonies; Germany and Italy are openly demanding a re-division; Japan is actually carrying it out in China, and the United States in Latin America.

To sum up: the possibility of extending the home capitalist market is strictly limited in the great capitalist countries. Voluntary increases in the share going to wages for the purpose of extending the home market is not to be considered by the capitalists. The growing luxury of the capitalist class is limited by the pressure towards accumulation. The transformation of farmers into agricultural capitalists on the one hand, and into proletarians on the other, has, in essentials, taken place. The workers' share of the product has began to show an absolute decrease. Export to independent countries comes up against tariff barriers, to the colonies against their monopolist rule by individual imperialist Powers; to the Soviet Union against the barriers of the foreign trade monopoly. The contradiction between production and the possibilities of realising goods on the market is growing greater. It will come to a head in a grave crisis, which will necessarily be but the prelude to a new war for the re-division of the world...

NOTES

1. Handbook of Labour Statistics, 1924-26. Issued by the American Department of Labour.
2. Statistical Abstract for U.S.A., 1926, p. 745.
3. To restore balance between production and sale the reformists are persuading the capitalists to pay higher wages in order to extend the buying capacity of the home market. Lenin has already answered this; it would be regarding the capitalists as blockheads if one seriously expected them unnecessarily to surrender a part of their surplus value to the workers merely in order to be able afterwards to sell the workers more commodities.

4. See table in Appendix.
5. "The necessity to export capital comes from the 'over-development' of capitalism in certain countries where (with agriculture backward and the masses impoverished) 'profitable' investments are becoming scarce."—(Lenin, "Imperialism," p. 71.)
6. See table in Appendix.

7

The Formation of Monopolies and the Struggle for the World Market

"Free competition leads to monopoly." This is one of Lenin's principal theses. Free competition, at a certain stage of development, must necessarily change into monopoly, because of concentration and centralisation. But

> "at the same time monopoly, which has sprung from free competition, does not drive the latter out of existence, but co-exists over it and with it, thus giving rise to a number of very acute and very great contradictions, antagonisms and conflicts. Monopoly is the transition from capitalism to a more highly developed order." (*Imperialism*, pp. 102-3.)

And it is true that in recent years we have witnessed an even greater concentration of concerns into monopolistic undertakings, both on a national and international scale.

It is unfortunately impossible to estimate at all reliably the extent of monopoly formation, the proportion of monopolies to total economy, and this for two reasons:

(1) The most complete form of monopoly—fusion—when the concerns which are being amalgamated completely surrender their independence and form an entirely new undertaking, is not fully dealt with in any statistics. The Steel Trust, or the International Dye-Stuffs Corporation, is today one concern, one monopoly, not a monopolist organisation.

It is a matter of economic history that it arose out of the fusion of many firms.

(2) On the other hand there are very effective monopolies that are not based on any formal, legal organisation. This is particularly the case in countries where there are legal obstacles to the formation of monopolies. Then, there are "gentlemen's agreements," unwritten associations, of which a breach is punished by boycott and other measures; for example, the famous "Gary dinners,"[1] the amalgamation of apparently independent concerns into one banking firm, where the uninitiated are not in the least aware that Mr. X. represents the interests of a large bank, etc.[2]

For these reasons it is not possible to compute the extent of monopoly statistically. But it is indisputable that in the great industrial countries, with the exception of England,[3] practically all important industries are already concentrated into monopolies, and that this process in recent years has been developing energetically.

A monopoly implies control of the market.[4] How does this come about? We may distinguish the following causes:

(1) Monopoly of capital— To start a new concern requires so much capital that it can only be managed with the assistance of the banks. Since, however, bank capital has grown up with the existing monopolies as finance capital, cooperation for the purpose of obtaining the capital is refused. If, in spite of that, a concern—usually not very strong financially—is started, it is not difficult for the monopoly, which has strong capital forces, to ruin it by a price war (e.g. the disappearance of independent cement firms because of the cartel in Germany).

(2) Monopoly in the sources of raw materials.— Apart from, or in conjunction with capital monopoly, a monopoly of raw materials is very important. This is particularly the case with regard to mines.

(3) Technical monopoly—With the progress in the chemical industry, a monopoly in technical knowledge is a

very important foundation for monopoly. Nowadays inventive work is rationalised, systematised and pressed into the service of large-scale capital. The International Dye Trust employs in its laboratories more than half of all the chemists in Germany. The same applies to many branches of the electrical industry and to the match industry, where the Swedish-American trust possesses all the patents; the position is similar in the machine-made shoe industry, where the American Trust has a monopoly based on the sole possession of a number of complicated machines.[5]

The best basis for a monopoly is the union of a monopoly in capital and technique, and this is the case with all the great monopolist organisations.

The object and purpose of forming a monopoly is to raise the profits of the concerns participating in it. This can be achieved:

(1) By raising the sale price above production price, selling at monopoly prices, e.g. appropriation of a larger share of total profits at the expense of unorganised capitalist and independent producers.[6]

(2) By reducing the cost of production through rationalisation; concentrating production on those works which produce most cheaply. Specialisation of firms in certain commodities, cutting down overhead expenses arising from competition, common employment of all patents and utilisation of technical experience, etc.

(3) By reducing the price of labour power below its value. The strength of trade unions, so long as they merely employ the peaceful strike as the method of struggle, is not great enough to defend the workers against powerful monopolies; the conditions of labour are automatically determined by monopoly capital.[7]

The form which the monopoly takes corresponds to the purposes enumerated above. We can differentiate between: Horizontal monopoly.—Amalgamation of concerns which produce the same commodities. The purpose here is to raise prices. There are various forms of such monopoly: simple price agreements, cartels to regulate all conditions of sale, quota cartels, trusts (financial cooperation by the mutual interchange of shares), etc., and complete fusion.

Vertical monopoly.— Amalgamation of concerns, of which the product of one serves as the raw material for another: coal, coke, iron, smelting works, machine factories, sawmills, cellulose, paper, artificial silk, etc. The object here is to adjust profits to compensate for the fall in the prices of various raw materials and semi-manufactured articles, and to reduce costs of production by systematic organisation of production from the raw material to the finished article.[8]

The economic difference is that horizontal monopoly wipes out rivalry in the commodities which it produces, while vertical monopolies exist side by side and may be in competition with each other at every stage of production, as was formerly the case with the vertical trusts in heavy industry.

The most recent form, the highest stage, is the super-monopoly, the horizontal amalgamation of vertical trusts, as exemplified in the German Steel Works and international Dye Trust, and in the Brunner Mond concern in England. The result is either a complete monopoly or a monopoly within the monopoly of the horizontal cartels controlled at every stage of production by the super-monopoly. For example, the German Steel Works Trust possesses concerns in the various monopolies existing in the different processes of heavy industry—iron, steel, wires, pipes—as much as approximately half of the total concerns, and is therefore in a position to influence the policy of the cartels to a proportionate extent. The power of such a super-monopoly is consequently extraordinarily great. They are very closely connected with the banks, and are the most completely developed form of finance capital. The huge profits raked in by the great monopolies are more or less hidden from the public eye. Firstly, a great part of the profits is reinvested in the concerns themselves. The American Steel Trust employed 115,000,000 dollars for purposes of extension in the last four years (this is the so-called "self-financing"). Dupont, chief shareholder in General Motors, Ltd., refers to a clear profit of 41,000,000 dollars for 1927 (after payment of preference interest). The share value of General Motors stands at 120,000,000 dollars, but on the Exchange it is valued at 539,000,000 dollars (*New York Times*, 28-1-28). When profits are so great capital is correspondingly increased. Courtauld's pays a 25 per cent dividend, and the capital is increased from £24,000,000 to £48,000,000 by the issue of bonus shares, and only 12 per cent is therefore paid in dividends. It is obvious therefore that nothing would be more incorrect than to determine actual profits by the dividend payments of monopolies.

The power of monopolies is so great that they exercise a decisive influence on the State and completely control economic policy. A new form of State capitalism is being evolved, which consists in serving the great monopolies. The State which they control serves their special interests; economic policy is placed at the service of monopolist price policy; foreign competition is excluded by means of protective tariffs, etc. We shall discuss this in the next chapter.

With regard to monopolies, the internal contradictions in the capitalist system of production show themselves in the following ways:

The further monopoly progresses, the more goods are sold at monopoly prices; the higher those monopoly prices become. In other words, since total profits cannot be greater than total surplus value, monopoly profits can only be won at the expense of the profits of capital not organised in the monopolies. The further monopoly progresses, the smaller the proportion of unorganised capital in the total capital of a society grows, the smaller becomes the possibility of appropriating monopoly profits. If total capital were divided among equally strong monopolies, there would be no more monopoly profits, but each form of capital would make the average rate of profit.[9]

Another contradiction: the immediate extent of a monopoly's power is the national State area; as far as the State power of the bourgeoisie extends, so far stretches the power of the national monopolies. Outside the State area there is competition among monopolies, expressed most sharply in the form of dumping. If the opposing monopolies are of equal strength, then dumping by both destroys the monopoly on the home market in spite of protective tariffs (if these latter are not absolutely prohibitive). Dumping and protective tariffs cancel each other out in their effects!

Limitation to the home demand, if there are protective tariffs, is possible only in the early stages of the development of an industry. As soon as the industry meets all the demands of the home market, monopolist capital is forced to dispose of a part of its production outside, in order to avoid surplus supplies on the home market whose capacity for absorbing the goods fluctuates according to the position of the industrial cycle. Sharp competition begins, leading eventually to the formation of super-national monopolies.

Super-national monopolies, embracing many countries, are already numerous, and the number is increasing. They are a super-organisation of the national monopolies, including a few or all countries. Sometimes there are two rival international organisations, such as Standard Oil and Royal Dutch; sometimes national monopolies in a few countries are amalgamated, while the same industry in other countries is still unorganised: the European Steel Cartel includes the Continental steel works, the American Steel Trust controls the American market, while the English steel industry is unorganised. In other instances a monopoly is directly controlled by the industry of other countries. (This is the case with the Swedish-American match trust.) There is a great variety in the forms of organisation, and conditions are constantly changing. Finance capital employs the most diverse methods of mutual conflict between firms in order, with a relatively small amount of capital, to gain decisive influence over a whole branch of industry.[10]

In general the basis of organisation consists in guaranteeing the home market for the national monopoly. In many cases foreign marketing are also divided among the national monopolies (e.g. the International Incandescent Lamp Cartel). Sometimes the association is valid only for a part of the world— "undisputed areas"—while competition proceeds in full force in the other parts of the world—"disputed areas."

There are also other forms. In those branches of industry where production is divided up among so many firms that the amalgamation of all the producers in the country into a monopoly organisation appears to be impossible, a situation occurring chiefly in agricultural production where there is a very numerous peasantry, a monopoly organisation can only be established by making a detour to cover trading capital. Only a part of the products destined for sale, and particularly that part which is to be exported, is appropriate as a basis for the formation of an international monopoly. So, for example, the wheat export of Canada, Australia and the Argentine is concentrated in monopolist organisations, for the purpose of raising wheat prices on the world market. In contrast to industry, a monopoly is in this case desired only for that portion of the product which is to be sold outside the national frontiers; prices on the home market rise only as a part of a general rise in the level of prices on the world market.

International monopolies are not very strong organisations. The struggle of the national monopoly for a larger share of the world market is carried on as a struggle for quotas or market spheres, or by secret underbidding, and destroys many of these organisations. Complete fusion into one concern, which could alone prevent such destruction, is rendered impossible because of the opposing interests of the national capitalist classes as a whole.[11] International cartels imply only a temporary armistice in the struggle for the world market.

For this reason all theories which accept international monopolies as the material foundation of a peaceful super-imperialism are essentially false. Lenin explained this in *Imperialism*:

> "Many bourgeois authors express the opinion that international cartels, as one of the most flexible manifestations of the internationalisation of capital, offer a hope of the maintenance of peace between the nations within capitalism. This view is theoretically completely unsound, and, in practice, a sophism, a dishonest way of defending the worst sort of opportunism."

At the present time it is the social democrats, above all Hilferding, who have adopted the theory, utterly destroyed by the world war, held by Norman Angell[12] and the free trade pacifists generally, the theory which is expressed in the catchword "realistic pacificism." This, however, does not by any means prevent them from most strongly supporting the claims of "their" bourgeoisie for a re-division of the world.[13]

The bourgeoisie itself is not at all so optimistic with regard to the effects of international monopoly as a means of ensuring peace. De Wendel recently showed, quite calmly, that even before the war a Franco-German iron cartel was in existence, but that did not prevent the outbreak of the war.[14]

Just so little can international monopolies help to prevent economic crises, as Hilferding believes, or seems to believe:

> "... A change in capitalism from free competition to organised capitalism is taking place. This is naturally accompanied by greater conscious order in and direction of economic life, which is trying to overcome the anarchy inherent in capitalism of the free competition type by capitalist methods... If this tendency could be carried into practice without obstacles... the instability arising from capitalist relations of production would be diminished, crises, or at least their reactions on the workers, would be ameliorated. Conditions of labour would assume a

> more constant character, unemployment would be less threatening, its consequences softened by insurance..."[15]

Experience shows that monopolies do not prevent crises; such could only be the case with a capitalist planned economy. The formation of monopolies frees the monopolists from the consequences of crises. In free competition capitalism, crises made themselves acutely felt by reducing the value of commodities which were produced in excess of the consumption capacity of society, by a sharp fall in prices to their socially necessary value. In these cases the capitalists bore the chief part of the cost in the form of property losses, bankruptcies, etc. Monopoly capitalism cannot do away with crises, i.e. with the contradiction between the productive forces of society and its consumption power determined by antagonistic relations of distribution. But monopolies are certainly capable of transferring the burden of crises from themselves, because they can maintain high prices even during a crisis, and bring about stability not by depreciating the value of surplus commodities, but by *limiting output*, that is, at the expense of the workers, at the same time being able to reduce to a level convenient for them. It is not credit crises, not bankruptcies, not bank failures which characterise the crises of monopoly capitalism, but permanent mass unemployment.[16] The reaction of the crises in the working class is not ameliorated under monopoly capitalism, as Hilferding maintains, but accentuated.[17]

The existence of international monopolies strengthens the position of capital as against the workers in the economic struggle. A labour dispute spread over a whole branch of industry in a country formerly threatened the capitalists concerned with heavy losses in the world market. If, however, strong international monopolies exist, with quotas or capital shares, the capitalists can carry on the struggle without regard to the world market. International monopolies therefore must be met by the internationalisation of trade union organisations and of the economic struggle.

Recapitulating we can say that the formation of monopolies on an international scale is a method of increasing the exploitation of the proletariat, of the unorganised capitalists and independent producers by financial capital. International monopolies mean a temporary and partial armistice among the national monopolies in their struggle for markets. Monopolies do not prevent either war or crises; they merely transfer the burden of crises from capital to the proletariat.

NOTES

1. Gary, the recently deceased president of the American Steel Trust, used, before the formation of the trust, to invite the leaders of the iron industry to dinner each month, and there agreements as to prices and production were reached.
2. Attempts to understand the formation of monopolies, such as the well-known memorandum of the German Economic Ministry, are of little value, because they are based on external characteristics.
3. It would be erroneous to believe that there are no powerful monopolies in England. In his valuable book ("Industrial Combination in England," London, 1927), P. Fitzgerald gives the following examples of monopolies:

Coats' Cotton Trust	£28,000,000
Cotton Dye Trust	10,000,000
Lever Bros.	64,500,000
Mond Chemicals	57,000,000
Royal Dutch Oil	70,000,000
Courtauld's Artificial Silk	32,000,000

This suffices to show that certain organisations are not far behind the largest German concerns, such as the International Dye Trust and United Steel Works, in capital strength. The formation of monopolies is rendered difficult by the absence of any general protective tariff, but has recently been making great progress (e.g. the Armstrong-Vickers fusion in heavy industry, district cartels in coal mining, formation of trusts in the cotton industry, etc.).

4. Control of the market does not mean that all firms which produce a certain commodity must be included in the monopoly. According to the kind of commodity and the situation of the market, 50 per cent to 80 per cent of total production is enough to give control of the market, and with agricultural products the supply of which can only be increased on the market after at least one or two years, even less than 50 per cent is often sufficient.
5. See E.J. Jones, "The Trust Problem in the U.S.A.," p. 165.
6. The agrarian crisis in so far as it is affected by the "scissors" and not by the rents fixed in the time of former high prices, is the most obvious expression of the appropriation of a part of the average profits of independent producers by monopoly capital.
7. Hilferding maintains ("Society," p. 291) that progress in the chemical industry is at the expense of heavy industry, and diminishes the antagonism between capital and labour.

   "It [the chemical industry] is not in such direct and immediate opposition to the working class as is heavy industry," because the share of wages is less, and such huge profits are made that, in comparison wages seem to decrease. "Actually, however, the chemical industry pays shamefully low wages, and is carrying out a policy of cutting down wages."
8. A degenerate form of such organisation was seen in the inflation concerns, when groups of capitalists bought up the stocks of bankrupt firms, e.g. the notorious Stinnes concern. Since they had no basis in technical production, they crumpled up with the stabilisation of the exchanges.
9. In general there is no price-cutting competition among horizontal monopolies; but there is a struggle between cartels producing different commodities which serve the same purpose, e.g. iron, tiles, cement, wood as building materials, coal, oil, wood, peat, water power as sources of energy. An excessive rise in the price of one of these tends to concentrate consumption on its substitutes. Modern technical development makes it much easier to replace one object by another. This places a limit on increase of monopoly prices.
10. See e.g. the "Economist" of 12-5-28, which describes the control exercised by Courtaulds over practically the whole

artificial silk industry of the world.

11. The International Holding Companies are an example of the highest stage of development; the shares of the concerns organised with a monopoly are transferred to another organisation, which issues its own shares in exchange. The profits of all the companies concerned are then pooled and distributed equally as a dividend on the shares of the holding company.
12. Norman Angell: "The Great Illusion," one of the most popular pacifist books of the pre-war period.
13. In one of Labriola's articles in "Gesselschaft," April, 1928, there is an utterly chauvinist representation of the interests of the Italian bourgeoisie.
14. The De Wendels are typical representatives of international capital. Before the war one brother was a member of the German Reichstag, the other of the French Chamber. Now, when Alsace-Lorraine is French, both brothers are members of the French Chamber. The one has become a French, instead of a German patriot.
15. Hilferding , "Problems of Today," "Gesselschaft," No. 1.
16. I referred to this change in the character of crises in the "Neue Zeit" before the war.
17. Sombart, even better than Hilferding, has recognised the uses of the market cycle for capitalism:

    "If capitalism succeeded, during the whole period of its ascendancy, in keeping wages within moderate limits in spite of the rapid increases in capital accumulations, thus safeguarding its own vital capacity and development, this was due... in no inconsiderable degree, to the actual market cycle. This ensures that, in times of boom, wages do not increase equally with surplus value, because of the rapid rise in prices; but it is also this market cycle which floods the labour market as desired, thereby creating the industrial reserve army, by a regular movement of contraction, by making some labour power unnecessary. This reserve army is an obstacle to rising wages."—(Sombart: "Economic Life in Expanding Capitalism." 1927, p. 586.)

8

State Capitalism

> "Capitalism, in its imperialist phases, arrives at the threshold of the complete socialisation of production. To some extent it causes the capitalists, whether they like it or not, to enter a new social order, which marks the transition from free competition to the socialisation of production. Production becomes social, but appropriation remains private. The social means of production remain the private property of a few."
>
> —("Imperialism," p. 22.)

State capitalism, in its nature, is an attempt on a capitalist basis to wipe out the contradiction between productive forces and production relations: an inadequate compromise, which cannot solve the contradictions!

If one reviews the economic activity of capitalist States historically, it can be asserted that such activity is greatest when the bourgeoisie are least able to overcome the contradictions of capitalism with their own forces. In the expanding period of European capitalism, the ideas of *laissez-faire* prevailed; during the world war, when the existence of the ruling classes was at stake, the economic activity of the State became all-embracing. After the conclusion of the war the destruction of State capitalism began; in recent years, when technical development gives a still stronger impulse to the socialisation of production and the contradictions of stabilisation become apparent, this tendency towards State capitalism is given additional strength.

We can express the contradiction between the forces of production and the relations of production in the following way; the interest of the bourgeoisie as a whole is in contradiction to the special interests of individual capitalist groups. In the interests of the bourgeoisie the necessity arises of socialising certain economic functions. This can occur by these functions being taken over by the organisation of the capitalist class, by the capitalist State and eventually by the municipal organisations. This was the case with certain economic functions which even before the war were exercised by the State, such as the regulation of weights and measures, the organisation of currency (central banks of issue were everywhere, with a few exceptions, either State institutions or under State supervision), and important parts of the traffic system, post, harbours, canals and in many countries railways also.

The twofold character of the capitalist State was shown in this, that not only those economic functions were socialised which, if left in the hands of private capitalists, would be a monopoly dangerous to the capitalist class as a whole; but the State also took over those functions which would not be profitable if exercised by private capitalists—road construction, canals and railways, which, if managed privately, would not pay (strategic railway lines, etc.).

Social politics is a particular form of State interference. Its class significance lies in this: firstly, to protect the working class, whose exploitation forms the basis of the entire system of capitalist production, from physically deteriorating as a result of immediate exploitation by individual capitalists; secondly, to protect the capitalist class rule as a whole, by concessions to the working class as a whole or to privileged sections of it.

The economy of war time, the highest stage reached by State capitalism, was similarly built up on this principle. With the existing shortage of commodities State regulation of the distribution of raw materials, of production and of labour forces was so organised as to prevent the special interests of individual capitalists putting any obstacles in the way of concentrating all forces for the purpose of carrying on the war in the interests of the bourgeoisie as a whole.

In the present period, when the struggle for markets is of decisive importance to the bourgeoisie, the chief function of State economic activity is to support the national bourgeoisie in this struggle. The entire foreign economic policy, and to some extent the home economic policy, is subordinated to this object; external economic policy in the form of protective tariffs, trading agreements and the struggle for colonies; internal economic policy in the form of supporting all measures which help to reduce costs of production. According to the strength of the capitalist system in the individual countries, according to whether capitalism in the country concerned is still progressing or has already entered a period of decline, important modifications occur in the direction and extent of State capitalist activity. In the United States, for example, State capitalist participation is directed mainly towards reducing costs of production, chiefly by the avoidance of waste, in the widest sense of the term. It is also aimed at protecting the home market against foreign competition by means of high protective tariffs and support and regulation of the imperialist expansion policy of capitalism. In Germany, on the other hand, State participation in economic life extends much further and embraces all aspects of economic and social life.

State activity in the economic life of a country can be divided into two kinds: mere regulative activity and economic activity proper, State capitalism in the narrower sense.[1] In the first case of regulative activity by the State the means of production remain the private property of the capitalists. The State merely regulates the production and distribution of goods, influencing the distribution of income by regulating prices and conditions of labour without actually appearing itself as a capitalist employer or itself owning the means of production. The influence which the State exercises, by taxation and the use of the State finances, on the distribution of income belongs to this category; 10 to 20 per cent of the national income passes through the hands of the State in this manner.

In State capitalism proper the State owns productive concerns and produces goods which are brought on to the market either in competition with private capitalists or together with them in a monopolist organisation, or else the State acts as a single monopolist. Two forms of State capitalism may be distinguished in this respect:

1. State undertakings which serve the interests of the bourgeoisie as a whole by withdrawing them from private monopoly (post, harbours, canals, etc.).
2. Ordinary business undertakings which are also being carried on by private capitalists, such as mines, factories, etc.

The extent to which the State directly participates in economic activity varies in different countries. It is greatest in Japan and Germany, least in the United States. A few figures will illustrate the importance of State economy in the total complex of national economic life. In Germany 2,501,000 persons are employed in the State service nationally and municipally, or on railways or postal services. This is 8 per cent of all wage earners in Germany, but actually the figure should be at least 10 per cent, for it does not include those "working members of families" whose numbers greatly swell the figure of agricultural workers in Germany; and further because it consists to a great extent of better qualified and higher-paid workers. It can be safely asserted therefore that 10 per cent of all wage earners in Germany are employed in socialised concerns.[2]

The same book from which the above figures are taken

gives the following estimate of property owned by the State, the federal States, municipalities and public corporations:

Railways	26	milliard marks
Communal works	5	" "
Post	1	" "
Other public property	20	" "
Total	52	milliard marks

Property held publicly amounts therefore to one-fifth or one-sixth of the total national property.

A calculation has also been made for England, which estimates the value of property held publicly at £2,754 milliards.[3] But the property of cooperatives is included in this estimate, and that cannot really be considered as the property of public corporations. In any case, this estimate shows that the total of non-private property is much greater in England than one is accustomed to believe.

Some problems arise with regard to these facts.

Firstly, is the present tendency towards an extension or a decrease in State capitalism? This question cannot be answered satisfactorily for all countries. In some, for example, France and the United States, the reaction against the war-time regulation of the national economic life still continues; former State undertakings are being transferred to private capital, and the regulative activity of the State limited in many respects. On the other hand, there can be observed an increase of State activity in the economic life of England, Germany and particularly of Italy, where the Fascist State is, in its regulative functions, encroaching more and more upon all spheres of economic life.

Taking world capitalism as a whole there is without doubt a tendency towards strengthening State capitalism. This is brought about by the necessity for socialising certain economic functions, such as power supply, a necessity which grows more urgent with increasing technical development; it is also brought about by the accentuation of class antagonisms in the different capitalist countries, which makes it essential for the bourgeoisie to concentrate their forces more strongly in their struggle against the workers; by the increasingly bitter struggle for the world market, which necessitates State support of the bourgeoisie in this struggle; by the necessity to concentrate all capitalist forces for the coming fight for the re-division of the world.

The second problem concerns the attitude of the different classes to this State capitalist development. It is clear that as long as capitalist domination exists, the State is and remains an organ of the capitalist class; in its economic activity, therefore, the State may indeed act in opposition to the interests of individual groups, but never against the interests of the entire capitalist class as a whole or of dominating monopolist capital. If we come across attacks directed against State interference by various capitalist groups we may be sure that the special interests of that group were not sufficiently considered in some concrete instance. It is a part of the anarchic character of capitalism that there is no general economic-political regulation which will satisfy all sections and groups of capitalists equally. That is why there are always some groups which for a time make a stand against State capitalist interference.[4]

In this connection the position of the capitalists in the different countries is of great importance. If the capitalist class feels itself to be strong socially, it is against State interference; if danger threatens its supremacy, it immediately turns to State capitalism. If a particular group of capitalists in a given economic situation can make high profits at the expense of other sections it is against State interference, while the other sections are for it. When markets are good, the feeling of the capitalists is opposed to State interference; when markets are bad they seek the assistance of the State and go so far as to demand State monopolies.

> "State monopoly in a capitalist society is never anything else than a means of guaranteeing the income of millionaires who are on the point of going bankrupt in one branch of industry or another."—(*Imperialism,* p. 39.)

But most important of all is the internal change in the character of State capitalism itself which has occurred in the last few years. This change reflects the fact that capital is being very definitely split up into two sections: finance capital organised in monopolies and unorganised small-scale capital. Accordingly the State today is no longer the State of the whole capitalist class, but the State of a small clique of monopoly capitalists. The State no longer represents the interests of the entire bourgeoisie, but the interests of a few monopolists.

This change in the economic basis is expressed in the disappearance of the formerly existing independence of the State machine as against individual capitalists. Powerful monopoly organisations have made the State subordinate to themselves and themselves direct State capitalist activity. The change is particularly clear in the sphere of politics and economic policy. In France, e.g. it was the large banks which consistently put obstacles in the way of the execution of the economic programme of the left bloc in the last parliament, and brought about the downfall of the left cabinet by deliberate acceleration of the depreciation of the French exchanges. This was kept up until a finance-capitalist government, under Poincaré, was brought into power, a change which suited them.

In Germany the great monopoly organisations openly control the economic policy of the State. The negotiations for the Franco-German trading agreement had no result until the French and German iron industrialists had concluded their private arrangements. In this private agreement it was laid down how much iron should be exported from France to Germany and under what tariff; also under what tariffs the products of the German iron manufacturing industry should be imported into France. Nominally this private treaty was concluded independently of the trading agreements; it was to enter into operation when the Governments succeeded in concluding a corresponding tariff agreement. But actually the position of dependence was the reverse; the arrangements of the monopoly capitalists were submitted to the respective governments and then issued publicly in legal form.

The same position was even more glaringly apparent in the case of the German-Japanese commercial treaty. A settlement of the treaty was constantly delayed by the Japanese prohibition on the import of German dyes. So a director of the International Dye Trust went to Japan, made a private treaty concerning dye supplies with the Japanese Government, assisted by the German Embassy there; and this agreement was quite simply incorporated in the German-Japanese commercial treaty.

The influence of monopoly organisations and capitalist groups on the economic policy of the United States is equally clear. It is quite easy to follow the work of the trusts in the fixing of tariffs. Foreign policy in the U.S.A. is in many cases directly determined by the interested capitalists. Lamonte, Morgan's business partner, travelled to Japan, discussed loans there, and decided American-Japanese relations. Morrow, a director of Morgan's, was sent as Ambassador to Mexico, and in a short time he succeeded in having the Mexican laws directed against American oil interests annulled, etc.

Summing up, we can say that State capitalism, State participation in the economic life of a capitalist State tends to grow as the contradictions between the forces of production and the relations of production grow, giving an impulse towards socialisation, as the general instability of the capitalist system increases, giving an impulse towards State concentration of forces. But the development does not follow a single course. According to the stage of development of the forces enumerated above, according to the growing strength or weakness of the bourgeoisie, development either progresses rapidly or temporarily retrogresses. State capitalism cannot of course solve the internal contradictions of capitalism. Reformist speeches concerning the overthrow of capitalism by means of State capitalism and economic democracy only serve the purpose of weakening working class resistance and the workers' will to fight.

NOTES

1. See Bukharin's report at the 15th Congress of the C.P.S.U. and Lapinsky's article in the "Communist International" for 1928, Nos. 11-12.
2. These figures are taken from Julius Hirsch: "Economics and Police." Berlin, 1926.
3. "Britain's Industrial Future," p.74.
4. For this reason the utterances of leading capitalists against State capitalism must not be taken too seriously. Such speeches were often heard in Germany in the recent period of good markets. Capitalist associations took up an unequivocal stand against the system of arbitration and the "exaggeration of social policy." The speech of J. Goldschmidt, of the Darmstadt and National Bank, is very characteristic: "In our time politics and economics have been drawn closer together than at any other period. But the natural limits of the State and of economics must not be done away with by a complete fusion; still less should the too great interference of one in the sphere of the other endanger the natural course of development. ...The State must return to its proper tasks, and must refrain from transforming a free economy into one manipulated by the State..." He then quotes approvingly Hallnach's observation: "The State and economics are at their best when they mutually preserve some distance between themselves." ("Böresen-Kurier," 13-2-28.)

9

The Struggle for the World Market: Agrarianisation and Industrialisation

Capitalism dissolved the pre-capitalist union of agriculture and industry by superseding the elements of industry formerly contained in peasant economy and the peasant household, by breaking up the peasant class and changing the peasants either into small agricultural capitalists or landless agricultural workers. (In so doing the small agricultural capitalists were subjected to the domination of large-scale capital through marketing and credit relations.) The division into "town" and "country" took a parallel course; the word "town" being used in the sense of centres of industry. The differentiation took place in all countries; western Europe became "the industrial workshop of the world," other parts of the world became sources of raw materials and food supplies.

> "On the other hand, the cheapness of the articles produced by machinery, and the improved means of transport and communication furnish the weapons for conquering foreign markets. By ruining handicraft production in other countries, machinery forcibly converts them into fields for the supply of its raw material. In this way India was compelled to produce cotton, wool, hemp, jute and indigo for Great Britain. By constantly making a part of the hands 'supernumerary' modern industry, in all countries where it has taken root, gives a spur

> to emigration and to the colonisation of foreign lands, which are thereby converted into settlements for growing the raw material of the mother country; just as Australia, for example, was converted into a colony for growing wool. A new and international division of labour, a division suited to the requirements of the chief centres of modern industry springs up, and converts one part of the globe into a chiefly agricultural field of production for supplying the other part which remains a chiefly industrial field." —(*Capital,* Vol. I, p. 453.)

But along with the antagonistic character of the capitalist mode of production, other counter tendencies are to be observed. The drawing in of a country into the capitalist world market facilitated the change of pre-capitalist forms of capital—commercial capital and loan capital—into industrial capital. Certain industries arose in agricultural countries because of advantages in situation: raw materials, partly worked up, cost less to transport. Concerns grew up for collecting and conserving raw materials, for organising transport, etc.

Because of these advantages of situations, contradictions sprang up between the interests of the industrial bourgeoisie as a class and the private interests of individual capitalists. It is to the advantage of industrial capital that no new industries should grow up in these countries which have hitherto bought finished goods. But it is often more profitable for the individual capitalist to establish his works in the country where the raw materials are found and the market is available, than to transport the raw materials to the home country and send the finished goods back again; that is, to have double transport expenses. And individual interests take precedence of wider interests: so the period of the export of capital began, which worked in a contrary direction to that of the division of the world into industrial and agricultural spheres. There came the period of the industrialisation of agrarian countries.[1]

The process of industrialisation was accelerated by the world war. The shortage of ships, high shipping costs and the shortage of industrial commodities in the belligerent countries themselves gave a great impetus to the development of industry in colonial agrarian countries. The lack of sufficient machinery and of skilled workers alone hindered this development.

Military requirements were an added factor in this process. With the shortage of ships it was impossible to meet the military demands of the colonies as formerly from the resources of the home country. British imperialism renounced its policy of putting obstacles in the way of the industrial development of India, and demanded its industrialisation in order to be able to equip the troops fighting in Asia.

After the end of the post-war boom, as soon as the machinery of production was again working in peace conditions, and the products of the European industrial countries again appeared on the markets of the agricultural countries, a grave crisis arose in the young industry of these countries. Many concerns, which blossomed suddenly in the war as though in hothouses appeared incapable of life and broke down.

But as industry developed in these countries there arose also a capitalist group, composed of home and foreign capitalists whose main interest lay in maintaining these new industries and making them profitable, and who were ready to defend them. The defence consisted in introducing protective tariffs for the industries.

The efforts to keep national industry going were supported by the interests of national defence. The experience of the war had shown—and the development in armaments since the war confirmed this—that without an industry of its own a country is powerless in time of war. Every country therefore tried to develop at home at least some industries among these necessary for war, by means of high protective tariffs.

At this stage the policy of power entered upon its rights. Subject colonies like Egypt, Korea, French, Africa, etc., have no possibility of carrying out an independent customs policy.

China's autonomy with regard to tariffs was greatly limited by the imperialists and the lowest Customs duties in the world were imposed on her. But all other States, however weak compared with the imperialist great Powers, tried their utmost to utilise the right of having an independent customs policy in order to create home industries. This is true of the British dominions.

The attempt of *small* States to create home industry was in many cases frustrated by the small capacity of the home market which was unable to absorb the full production of a really modern concern. Small and inferior factories were constructed. A protectionist policy in small States meant consequently an obstacle to the free development of productive forces. On the other hand, the existence of industrial tariffs intensified the contradiction between the class interests of the bourgeoisie in preventing industrialisation—where the capacity of the home market was great enough—and the particular interests of individual capitalists in establishing production in countries protected by tariffs.

After stabilisation, when a market for industrial commodities became the great problem of the European industrial countries, a new politico-economic campaign against the protective tariff system of the agricultural countries was begun.[2] We may call to mind the famous Bankers' Manifesto which contained a warning against "artificial industrialisation", and demanded the abolition of protective tariffs, and of the sharp refusal with which it was met in Poland, Italy and even America.

In the same way the free trade decision of the World Economic Conference remained ineffective in practice. Protective tariffs were nowhere reduced, while artificial promotion of the growth of industry continued everywhere.

We cannot speak of a tendency towards agrarianisation in the sense of a positive decline of industry in agricultural countries. The process can be demonstrated by the relevant figures (see table in the Appendix).

The textile industry has made absolute progress in most colonial countries and in the less highly industrialised European countries. The employment of machinery has attained more or less the same level in colonial countries. In some countries it is higher, in a few lower than it was before the war.

If we consider the production of iron and steel the development is less uniform. There is a marked increase of production in Japan, British India and Australia, and an absolute decrease in Canada. Still, it would be quite false to infer from that a decline in the industrialisation of Canada. Special factors must be considered: the local advantages of highly developed American heavy industry are so great that it does not pay to create a domestic heavy industry by artificial means, still less as there is no question of war between Canada and the U.S.A.

The machine industry still remains a monopoly of European and North American industry, so that the "new" countries are still dependent upon the "old" industrial countries for their equipment with means of production.[3] In general, development has proceeded in such a manner that it is chiefly the more primitive staple industries, dealing directly with raw materials, which are developing, e.g. the coarse cotton industry among textiles. The finer branches of industry require more skilled workers, technique and a larger market than those possessed by agricultural countries; the latest technical achievements, the most skilful methods of production, are employed in the old industrial countries.[4]

The statistics available do not afford a basis on which to decide which of the two tendencies is stronger, that towards agrarianisation, or that towards industrialisation. It is, moreover, extremely difficult to find an exact and scientific method for deciding such a question. Statistics of employment are not applicable. In some cases there are none, in others they do not go beyond 1920, while some actually obscure the real process.

India is typical of this. The statistics of employment in

India show that for fifty years there has been a decrease in the number of those engaged in industry and an increase in the number of those engaged in agriculture; as far as we know, this is the only country which issues such statistics. Does this mean the agrarianisation of India? By no means! For although the number of workers engaged in the old primitive handicrafts is *decreasing*, large-scale industry of a modern capitalist type is developing.[5] There is no doubt that India today, in spite of the relative decrease in the number of industrial workers, is a more industrialised country than it was 50 years ago.

We might, also employ the method of "weighing" agriculture and industry as wholes. But apart from the difficulties of measurement—only the U.S.A. statistics are suitable for this—the following must also be taken into account. In many countries—Canada, Argentine, Australia, there is a twofold development in progress at the same time—a great expansion of agriculture by the development of hitherto unused areas, and the development of capitalist industry. It is possible that in these cases agricultural production grows more rapidly than industrial. Nevertheless, there would not, economically, be any sense in describing the results of these two parallel processes simply as "agrarianisation."

Summing up: the tendency is free competition capitalism to transform colonies into areas producing raw materials and foodstuffs for western Europe, the industrial workshop of the world, came up against a strong counter tendency in the period of imperialism, that of capital export, protective tariffs, war considerations. The difficulty of disposing of industrial commodities in the post-war period gave rise to the attempt on the part of industrial capitalism among the imperialist Powers, to force a policy of agrarianisation on the smaller States. This attempt was brought to grief by the contradiction between the class interest of the industrial bourgeoisie and the private desire of individual capitalists for profits, and by the opposition of the capitalists of the small independent countries, of the dominions and semi-colonies; it could only be fully thrust upon the colonies. Although there is no scientific method for deciding the question, we believe that it is not true to speak simply of agrarianisation; that, on the contrary, the tendency towards industrialisation is stronger than that towards agrarianisation.

NOTES

1. This tendency was, as far as I know, first described by the well-known German socialist-patriot G. Hildebrand in his book published before the war; "Industrial Supremacy and Industrial Socialism." He takes up a stand against this development and for capitalist colonial policy. He was at that time excluded from the German Social Democratic Party, but, after socialist-patriotism had become the official policy of that party, was again admitted into its ranks.
2. United States industry still produces mainly for the home market. The following percentages of total production were exported:

1899	1904	1909	1914	1918	1921	1923	1925
6.5	5.8	4.8	6.2	8.8	6.2	7.3	7.8

   (For 1925 a new method of calculation was used, excluding the double reckoning of raw materials. The figure, therefore, is actually higher for that year. See "Commerce Year Book," 1926, p. 92.)
3. World machine production was divided as follows in 1925: U.S.A. 57.6%; Great Britain 13.6%; Germany 13.1%; all other countries 15.7%. The share of these three countries in world production **rose** by 3.4% since 1913. See "The Machine Industry of the World," issued by the Association of German Machine manufacturers for the World Economic Conference.
4. This fact has led to the optimistic theory being put forward according to which the industrialisation of agrarian countries involves no injury to the economy of the old industrial countries, for the loss of staple industries is compensated for by an increasing demand for machines and other goods essential for a highly developed technique. The difficulties of British industry prove the falseness of this theory.
5. See Economic Review for the first quarter of the year 1928—"Inprecorr" Special Number.

10

Preparations for a Redivision of the World

> "The capitalists divide up the world, not because of original sin, but because the degree of concentration which has been reached forces them to take this road in order to get profits. And they divide it in proportion to capital, to "strength" because there cannot be any other system of division in a system of commodity production and capitalism." —(Lenin: "Imperialism," p. 85.)

The contradiction between the sham ideological struggle against war and the actual preparations for war is one of the basic facts of recent years. The pacifists of all shades of opinion, and above all the Social Democrats, wish to make the world believe that the world war was an "historical accident," brought about by the militarist policy of monarchs and by a false conception on the part of the bourgeoisie of their own class interests. Now, however, the age of super-imperialism, of "realistic pacifism" is approaching. Its economic bases are international cartels, international trustification, capital export, the closely interwoven interests of the bourgeoisie of the whole world. The League of Nations is its organisation; its instruments the treaties of peace, the non-agression pacts, and, latest of all, the all-embracing treaty of the "Outlawry of War."

But as against all these paper treaties and pretty speeches we can see the actual, iron reality of war preparations. The United States, which sponsors the idea of outlawing war, is at the same time building warships to the value of hundreds of million dollars; all States, without exception, are ceaselessly piling up armaments for the next war.

We must not be deceived by the Washington naval agreement. It deals with limitations on the construction of battleships, whose value as against the most modern fighting units—small cruisers, submarines and aircraft, has been called into question; with a very costly weapon (a modern battleship costs more than a hundred million dollars); America's threat to compete in the construction of warships forced the financially weaker competitors to give way on this question. The attempt to place a limit on the construction of cheaper types of ships was utterly defeated by the three greatest Powers at the Geneva Conference, after which France and Italy refused to take any part whatever in the Conference.

The fact that standing armies today are smaller than before the war is of just as little importance. As against that, technical equipment is incomparably better. Armies have become mechanised. Tank regiments have taken the place of cavalry, machine-guns the place of single weapons, etc. The League of Nations Disarmament Conference was very busy finding new excuses for preventing any genuine tackling of the disarmament problem... All pacifist ideas, disarmament conferences and talk of the outlawry of war, are nothing but manoeuvres intended to obscure the facts and to deceive the workers who detest war, and to produce the illusion of everything possible having been done to prevent war...

The reasons which Lenin adduced for the inevitability of war in the imperialist stage of capitalism apply with equal validity to the present period of capitalist decline. It is unnecessary to restate them. *But it is necessary to give a short sketch of the position and policy of the Powers at the present time.*

This picture is in part simpler, in part more complicated,

than that of the pre-war period. After the war Germany, Austria-Hungary and Tsarist Russia were no longer included in the ranks of the imperialist Powers. Only four independent imperialist World Powers remained: the U.S.A., the British Empire, Japan and France.[1] To that extent the picture is simpler. It is more complicated for the following reasons.

(1) Germany, because of its population and economic importance one of the leading countries of the world, was disarmed after the war, and was deprived of the possibility of imperialist activity. Nowadays Germany combines the characteristics of an imperialist Power with those of a colonial country. The economic substructure is imperialist —except for the import of capital, which was forced on Germany by reparation obligations; her disarmament carried out (at least officially), her obligation to pay reparations, foreign control and imports of capital are the characteristics of a colony.[2] The German bourgeoisie were driven by economic conditions to take up imperialist activities. They are openly propounding the question of the return of the German colonies. They are trying to find a place for themselves in the industry of French colonies.[3] They are again building railways in Turkey and Persia. Nevertheless Germany is not an imperialist country in the full sense of the word but a peculiar and contradictory structure: half an imperialist Power, half a colony under the control of imperialist Powers.

(2) Because of progress in military technique and because of the super-power of the four World Powers it has become impossible for the smaller countries to conduct an independent foreign policy, although they are nominally independent. Their foreign policy consists merely in steering between the imperialist Great Powers and exploiting their antagonisms. The peculiar aspect of this is that these countries include those with extensive colonial possessions! Holland, which cannot itself defend its own colonies, and relies upon England's protection; Portugal, which, although possessing colonies, has itself sunk into being a semi-colonial possession

of Great Britain; and finally Belgium, which is internationally protected and is adjacent to the domain of French power.

(3) The distinctions between independent States, colonies and semi-colonies are fast disappearing. Greece, for example, nominally independent, is actually more dependent upon England than are the British Dominions, The allegiance of Canada or Australia to the British Empire is purely a question of convenience for the capitalists of those countries. Were they to decide on secession, it is scarcely possible that the British bourgeoisie could make any attempt to compel them to remain within the Empire by force of arms.

(4) A twofold process is going on with regard to the relations between colonies and semi-colonies and the imperialist Powers. The formerly independent States of southern and central America are rapidly becoming dependent upon the United States, which is in this case playing a progressive role, in so far as the U.S.A. furthers capitalist development and supports the bourgeoisie against the feudal owners of land (on which England relies in these areas); at the same time the U.S.A. is bringing these capitalists and the countries themselves under its own sway.

The centrifugal development of the British Dominions within the Empire and the growing opposition of the old colonies and semi-colonies to imperialist oppression is in sharp contradiction to the trend of affairs in America. This opposition has in a few cases (Turkey and Afghanistan) resulted in complete success. In the case of China it has led to a temporary strengthening of imperialist domination (the open penetration of Japan into north China).

(5) The picture is still further complicated by inter-Allied debts and reparations; and finally by the existence of the Soviet Union as the magnetic centre of all anti-imperialist forces; a subject which we have already discussed.

We shall now deal with the characteristics of the principal imperialist World Powers.

The United States has in the last decade grown into a

fully developed imperialist State; but some features of the former period still remain. America still exports a great quantity of foodstuff. The home market is still of overwhelming importance; only six per cent of the industrial products are exported. American finance capital has not yet developed banking organisations abroad. Certain legal and ideological remains of the earlier period still hinder the free development of imperialist activity. But all such vestiges of the earlier period are being rapidly discarded. Technical development is out-distancing the extension of the home market, mass unemployment is in existence, the export of commodities and capital, and monopolised areas to which to export have become an economic necessity.

The sphere of imperialist activity for the U.S.A. is primarily the American continent. The lands bordering the Caribbean Sea have openly been proclaimed as a sphere where the U.S.A. has "special interests." The protection of the Panama Canal serves as the justification of this proclamation. The rest of South America comes under the Monroe doctrine which is similarly interpreted to meet the requirements of American imperialism. The South American States are daily growing more dependent upon the U.S.A. economically, financially and politically (e.g. the Pan-American Conference). Canada, nominally a part of the British Empire, is being more and more drawn into the sphere of American economic life....

The superiority of the U.S.A. in the American continent is economically and militarily unassailable. The U.S.A. is, and remains, before all, an American Power.

The British Empire, apart from Canada, surrounds the Indian Ocean. England is principally an Indian Ocean Power. Around India there is Outer India (Singapore), Australia, New Zealand and Africa. Egypt, Mesopotamia, Palestine, Gibraltar and Malta guard the road to India. England's gains in the war, in near Asia and East Africa, served to round off and complete her rule over the Indian Ocean. (Motor communication direct from the Mediterranean to Bagdad and India; uninterrupted land routes from Cape Town to Cairo.) But while imperialism in the U.S.A. is on the upgrade, that of England—in spite of the new possessions gained by the war—is going downhill. The great settlement colonies of Canada and Australia are turning towards the United States. The revolt of the workers in the downtrodden colonial and semi-colonial areas is growing stronger, in spite of the fact that the leading capitalists have for the most part aligned themselves with the imperialists in those countries where the national revolutionary movement is developing into an anti-capitalist movement.

Japan is a Far Eastern Power. It is much weaker than the Anglo-Saxon World Powers. It is partly dependent economically on the U.S.A., which buys the greater part of the silk exports which are so important to Japan and exports capital to that country. Its existence as a capitalist Power depends mainly on China. Being itself weak in raw materials, it can only carry on its industry with the help of its colonies —Korea, Manchuria, Shantung, Formosa, and of China itself.

France is predominantly a Mediterranean-African Power (although it possesses a valuable colonial area in Indo-China also). The African colonies lie near to the motherland, and are most closely bound to her economically and strategically. France's weakness is in her small and stagnant population; her strength in her military superiority on the continent. Politically and militarily she is closely connected with Poland, Yugoslavia, and Czechoslovakia, (the economic connection is not very important), but taken as a whole France is also much weaker than the two Anglo-Saxon World Powers.[4]

Between these four World Powers, which independently conduct an imperialist world policy, the other States vacillate here and there in changing alliances and blocs in so far as they are not already appendages of one of the World Powers. The decisive factor in this connection is the growing rivalry of the World Powers called into existence by their struggle for markets, raw materials and the possession of monopolised areas. This rivalry is at present at its sharpest between the two greatest World Powers, England and the U.S.A. It extends over the whole world; in South America, Canada, Australia, China, everywhere American Capital is pressing hard upon English capital, demanding the "open door" for all areas which it controls, demanding, that is, equal rights. The struggle is also directed against the monopoly in raw materials which British finance capital has achieved: rubber, tin, etc. The struggle over oil—Royal Dutch against Standard Oil— is a vital factor in this antagonism. American armaments are directed principally against Britain's sea supremacy which still exists in spite of the Washington Agreement, since England possesses naval bases everywhere and owns an overwhelming number of merchant vessels which in the event of war could be used as auxiliary cruisers.[5]

There is also continuous antagonism between the U.S.A. and Japan. The U.S.A. is demanding the "open door" in China, which it considers to be the best future market. Apart from that there is rivalry over the hegemony of the Pacific Ocean. The U.S.A., at the Washington Conference thrust Japan out of China and compelled England to sever her alliance with Japan.

France and England are permanent rivals for superiority on the European continent. By the changes in war technique, England has ceased to be an island in the strategic sense of the term. French guns, with long distance ranges, can reach the English coast from the mainland. Aircraft can reach and bombard London in an hour. Submarines—as a result of the greater nearness of the bases and their greatly superior construction—can endanger England's shipping to an incomparably greater extent than did the German submarines during the war, submarines which were both less numerous and more primitive than those of today. In the same way there is a deep antagonism between France and Germany—in spite of the many international monopolies. Germany will, within a short time, have a population twice as great as that of France, and is developing more rapidly than France both technically and economically. The fear of a war of revenge is one of the chief factors governing French foreign policy, in spite of Locarno, Thoiry, and all peace guarantees.

The military supremacy of France forces England to seek allies on the Continent. This explains her good relations with Italy which is herself strongly opposed to France. The basis of Franco-Italian antagonism is the fact that in the re-division of the world at the close of the war Italy came out worse than any other of the victorious States, because she had shown herself to be the weakest. The spoils intended for Italy in Asia Minor were lost because of the national re-birth of Turkey. That is why the North Italian industry which developed so rapidly is urgently in need of a good position on the world market and of colonies, the Italian home market being particularly small. But the world is divided up. Italy has only received worthless crumbs. The obvious sphere of Italian imperialist expansion would be around the Mediterranean. But wherever Italy turns, she comes up against France.[6] Almost in sight of Sicily lies Tunis, a French possession, where there are more Italians than French. Towards the East, Italy, in its drive towards expansion, comes up against Yugoslavia, which is supported by France. Italy is, therefore, a willing tool in the hands of England for her struggle against France. Apart from Italy, England seeks to strengthen Germany as a counterpoise to France—with whom, by the way, the Entente Cordiale still exists. But Germany is England's greatest rival in the industrial sphere, political interests are therefore in conflict with immediate economic interests.

It would take us to eternity even to enumerate all the antagonisms which divide the Balkans and eastern Europe; Germany against Poland; Hungary against Romania, Yugoslavia and Czechoslovakia; Poland against Lithuania; Bulgaria against Yugoslavia, etc. These antagonisms are expressed in the most diverse alliances. Such blocs are however shortlived; the internal opposition of interests is continually demolishing them, or they neutralise each other. The foundations of alliances are, for example, the following:

> (*a*) The universal hostility of all capitalist States to the Soviet Union. This bloc is always latently in existence. But the opposition of interests is so strong that up to the present it has not materialised, England's efforts to unite all the central and east European States into a bloc for an attack on the U.S.S.R. have not yet succeeded, because these attempts themselves bring to light all the latent hostilities in eastern Europe.
>
> (*b*) The common hostility of all colonial powers to the colonies and semi-colonies oppressed by them—a subject we have already discussed.
>
> (*c*) The common hostility of all European debtor States to their master creditor, the U.S.A.
>
> (*d*) The common hostility of all the victorious countries, interested in maintaining the status quo, to the defeated countries which were destroyed or despoiled in the war.
>
> (*e*) The common interest of all reparations creditors in the operation of the Dawes Plan.[7]
>
> (*f*) There is a bloc of the States surrounding Hungary—the Little Entente—to protect their possessions. There is another bloc arising, cutting right across it, composed of Fascist States: Italy, Hungary, Poland, Bulgaria, Romania.

But all this is unstable, changing, brittle. The hostile interests of the world powers disintegrate all these changing alliances, force their policies on the small States, which, exploiting the hostile interests of the powers, are trying to attain a relative independence.

To sum up: the present political relations of power are determined by the opposition of the capitalist world to the Soviet Union, by the hostility of the imperialist Powers to the colonies, and by the clash of interests among the imperialist Powers themselves (U.S.A.-England; U.S.A.-Japan; England-France). The smaller States, nominally independent, have either become mere appendages of the world Powers or are at any rate incapable of carrying out an independent policy. Finance capital among the Great Powers is uninterruptedly preparing for a war to re-divide the world, and the small States, willy nilly, will have to take part. There will be fewer neutral States in the next war than there were in the last! League of Nations, disarmament conferences, pacts of non-agression, outlawry of war, etc., are partly deliberately deceptive manoeuvres, partly expressions of the capitalist fear of the consequences of a new world war, which would certainly end with the overthrow of the capitalists' regime in a number of countries. That is why the bourgeoisie is anxious to defeat the dictatorship of the proletariat in the U.S.S.R. before the fight begins among themselves, in order to deprive the revolutionary workers of the world of their organised centre of power.

NOTES

1. See the table in appendix: "The Great Powers of the World."
2. In spite of official disarmament, Germany is by no means defenseless. There exist technically well-equipped and well-formed divisions of officers and subalterns which, in the event of war can be immediately changed into a great army if supplemented by trained man power. Germany has extensive civil aviation which can also be used for military purposes in a very short time; it has the best developed chemical industry of the world. Potentially, there is the possibility of constructing tanks in a very short time out of finished motors and armour plates, with the assistance of the engineering industry. What is lacking, and what cannot be improvised, is heavy artillery and ships.
3. Early in February, 1921, the French senator Lemery negotiated in Berlin for the establishment of Franco-German trading companies to exploit the French colonies.
4. In particular France's communications with her African colonies are constantly threatened by the sea-power of Britain which possesses powerful naval bases at Gibraltar and Malta.
5. The disputes at the Geneva Naval Disarmament Conference,

which were difficult for the lay mind to understand, revolved around the maritime rights of England in the event of a war, around the question of the "freedom of the seas." America, being short of naval bases and merchant ships wanted to fix the type of "small cruisers" and their equipment in such a manner as to make them superior to England's merchant vessels used as auxiliary cruisers. England was determined on a smaller type with less armaments in order to be able, in the event of war, to wage battle against small foreign cruisers with her auxiliary cruisers. For Japan, which is interested only in China, the point was one of indifference; she could therefore play the part of mediator.

6. The Mediterranean is important for England not as a colonial area, but as the road to India. England holds the most important strategic points Gibraltar, Malta, etc., but apart from Egypt and Palestine has no colonies there.
7. As on all other points, the interests of the separate national capitalist classes, and the sections within these classes, are in opposition. For England, reparations are not a very important financial affair; the chief desire is to exchange the reparation payments against her debts to America. But for France reparation imports are very important. Finance capital in the U.S.A. is mainly concerned with guaranteeing its capital investments in Germany, and is therefore in favour of a revision of the Dawes Plan, but refuses to cancel inter-allied debts for this purpose, although they are not of great financial importance to America. Since, moreover, reparation payments can, in the long run, only be made by a greatly increased export of German industrial products, which would seriously injure the industrial interests of the receiving countries, there is a sharp division among the capitalists of those countries. That is why reparations cannot serve as a lasting foundation for the formation of alliances.

11

Present-day Capitalism as Viewed by the Reformists

The world situation, which we outlined in the preceding chapter, shows the instability of the capitalist system, its inherent and fundamental contradictions. It is true that the great revolt of the working class, the attempt to destroy the capitalist system in Europe after the war ended with the defeat of the proletariat and the stabilisation of capitalism, because of the cunning manoeuvres of the bourgeoisie, the treachery of the social-democrats and the absence of Communist Parties. But the decay of capitalism has nevertheless begun. Capitalism could not regain its mastery over the whole world—one-sixth of the globe is lost to it; the proletariat rules in the U.S.S.R.! The contradictions within the capitalist world are more marked. In the central capitalist areas the transformation of independent producers into petty capitalists or workers is almost completed. Those workers who become unemployed as a result of technical progress no longer find work, as hitherto, in the expansion of the capitalist market. The result is permanent mass unemployment, accompanied by the idleness of a great part of the machinery of production and the increased exploitation of a small number of workers.

Concentration and centralisation are continuing. The

growth of monopolies is increasing by leaps and bounds. A small group of the most important capitalists who are at the head of the monopolies and banks, direct economics and politics. From time to time they continue to form international monopolies and divide the world market between them.

The contradiction between social production and private appropriation becomes ever keener and more intolerable. The State is becoming a tool of the monopolies; bourgeois democracy can no longer conceal the contradictions; in its place there is growing up, to an ever greater extent, the system of capitalist terror as a permanent institution—Fascism.

The rivalry of the world Powers, the competition for markets and for the possession of monopoly spheres—in spite of international monopolies—the hostility to the U.S.S.R., all these factors lead to the maddest competition in armaments, to violent new world wars, the extent of which it is impossible to foresee.

Only the overthrow of capitalist supremacy, which can only occur by means of an armed struggle, by the destruction of the bourgeois State—and not by any peaceful evolution—can save humanity.

What do the reformists say to this? What picture of the world do they present to the workers?

It is not easy to answer these questions. The theories of the reformists appear in many hues, contain versions of all bourgeois theories veiled in sham Marxist phraseology, and often deliberately shelve the problem. Besides, the same contradictions that exist between the capitalist classes of different countries are also to be found among the various social democratic parties since they form the extreme left wing of the capitalist parties as a whole. In the following we shall deal principally with Hilferding, for in spite of his degeneracy, he has the clearest head of all the reformists.

This reformist world picture is approximately as follows:

(*a*) *The present period is not one of capitalist decline.* The separation of the U.S.S.R. from the capitalist world does not indicate the beginning of the end of the capitalist system. There has not been a *proletarian,* but a *bourgeois-peasant* revolution. The Bolsheviks, as the ruling party, are obliged to consider the interests of the peasantry as the strongest "social force" (Otto Bauer). The social and economic system of the Soviet Union is not a socialist one, but a primitive capitalist one. Not the proletariat, but a small clique *above* the proletariat, rules in the Soviet Union. The liberation of the proletariat necessitates the fall of the Bolshevik Government. (Kautsky).

(*b*) *Capitalism is approaching a new period of expansion.* "Does this crisis in capitalism," asks Hilferding, "really mean, as so many say, the end of normal capitalist development, or does it indicate, as Professor Harms thinks, a new boom in capitalism? Actually, Professor Harms has already demonstrated this new expansion to us, for if one does not limit oneself to any particular national considerations, all the facts which he enumerates are nothing but the foundations of the revival of a vastly-extended world capitalism." — (*Report of the Vienna Social and Political Union,* 1926.)

(*c*) *Capitalism today differs from earlier forms of capitalism because it is organised and planned.* "The era of free competition, in which capitalism was governed solely by blind laws, is being superseded by the capitalist organisation of economy, that is, we are faced with organised economy instead of with a blind play of forces..."

Organised capitalism means... the replacement of the capitalist principle of free competition by the socialist principle of regulated production. (Report to the Kiel Congress.)

(*d*) *The action of the State is, in the period of organised capitalism, of decisive importance to the fate of the working class.*

"The better the organisation.... the more intolerable for the mass of producers grows the usurpation of economic power and of social products by the owners of amalgamated and concentrated means of production... The contradiction disappears through the change in economy from being hierarchically to being democratically organised. Conscious social regulation of national economy by the few for their own purposes becomes regulation by the mass of producers. Capitalism is setting itself the problem of economic democracy... its establishment is a long historical process in which concentrated capital becomes increasingly subject to democratic control." (*Die Gesellschaft.*)

(*e*) *The State today is not an instrument of capitalist domination.* Marx certainly gave the State a distinguishing characteristic by saying that the State should not only be considered as a political body, but also according to its social function, which consists in maintaining the supremacy of the ruling classes by means of the State power. But this definition of the State by Marx is not by any means a theory of the State, for it applies to all State forms since the beginning of class societies, and we must therefore elucidate the distinguishing characteristics of State development.... The State is nothing but the Government, the machinery of administration and the citizens who compose the State.... In other words, this means that the essential elements of any modern State are the parties, because the individual can only realise his will through the medium of the party. Consequently all parties are necessary component parts of the State, in the same way as the government and the administration... (*Kiel Report.*)

The necessity of a coalition government is an evident consequence of this, in order to be able to influence the State and to overcome with the help of the State, the contradiction between political freedom and economic slavery.

(*f*) *The transition from capitalist rule to socialism will not be brought about by the collapse of capitalism, but by the gradual attainment of economic democracy.*

"The idea that the collapse of capitalism will automatically take place because there will no longer be any precapitalist markets, can be rejected as erroneous. I believe that in this I am in complete agreement with the teachings of

Karl Marx, to whom a theory of collapse is always falsely attributed. The second volume of *Capital* shows that production within the capitalist system is possible on an overexpanding scale. I have often thought that it is not altogether regrettable that the second volume should be so little read, for in certain circumstances, a panegyric of capitalism might be extracted from it." (Loud laughter and cries of "Quite right!") (*Social Political Union.*)[1]

In order to accomplish the change from an economy organised and directed by capitalists into an economy directed by the democratic State, democracy, and the political power of the working class, to be gained by democratic means and aiming at economic democracy, is necessary.

(*g*) *Democracy today is not "bourgeois" democracy.*

"It is historically false and misleading to speak of bourgeois democracy.... Considered historically, the proletariat has always championed the cause of democracy.... *We* had to wrest it from the rulers in a stiff fight.... the rulers must now turn to the citizens and have their rule continually ratified by a majority in lively conflict with us."

Should the bourgeoisie attempt to ignore the democracy, this would lead to the use of violence in the class struggle, to a long-drawn-out, most embittered and extremely costly civil war. If the foundations of democracy are destroyed, the working class is put on the defensive and has no choice but to use whatever means are at its disposal. But social democracy will not turn to civil war as long as democracy is assured, for it realises that... "there is no graver obstacle to the realisation of socialism than civil war, and because we, as socialists, would find ourselves in an extremely difficult position if the proletarian State power were to arise out of civil war. That is why we, as the proletariat, have so strong an interest in the maintenance of democracy." (*Kiel Congress.*)

"The catchword of formal democracy is incorrect. Democracy implies a changed distribution of political power. It implies other social effects, and implies also that the will of the State is likewise differently fashioned. It is, therefore quite false to say that democracy is formal; it is of the greatest real importance in the fate of all the working classes. If there are illusions to be destroyed today they are not those which Marx destroyed in 1848. Today it is not the democratic, but the anti-democratic illusions which are dangerous."

(*h*) *The immediate object of the workers is the struggle for economic and factory democracy.*

"Economic democracy means the subordination of private economic interests to social interests; factory democracy is the possibility for each individual to rise to the leadership of the concern, according to his capabilities." (*Kiel Report.*)

What is actually meant by "economic democracy" it is impossible, with the best will in the world, to determine, although so much has been written on the subject. The various reformists understand quite different things, but all are somewhat vague; participation in the management of monopoly concerns by means of the introduction of State councils, composed of capitalists, workers, and consumers (Otto Bauer), influencing economic policy by the socialist parties participating in the government; economic democracy by means of trade unions and factory committees; workers sharing in the profits of the capitalists by means of workers' shares, profit-sharing, etc.; the supersession of capitalism by the concentration of workers' savings in cooperatives, workers' concerns, etc.—all these are parts of the entirely vague idea of economic democracy.

By factory democracy is obviously meant the equal rights of the workers to decide on the appointment and dismissal of workers, the determination of conditions of labour, etc.

(*i*) *Since capitalism still has a long lease of life, since it should not be destroyed but is to evolve into socialism, rationalisation must be supported.*

"We need a powerful, and not a decadent, impoverished capitalism, for it is to the advantage of the inheritors if their inheritance is as great as possible."—(Hilferding, *Social Political Union.*)

It is only necessary that the workers should receive a proportionate share of the greater production which results from rationalisation; that, at least, their share of total production should not decrease.[2]

"This is even more necessary in order to prevent capitalism from experiencing great difficulties because of the narrowness of the market."

"A larger share of the total must reach such persons as will presumably use it for purposes of consumption. A greater part of the product must fall to the workers. Higher wages are advantageous to capitalism itself." (Tarnov, *Why Be Poor?*)

(*j*) *The increase in the number of international monopolies is the foundation of realist pacifism, of superimperialism.*

International monopolies bring order into the capitalist system. The organised distribution of markets makes war superfluous and stupid for economic reasons. The League of Nations is the political expression of this combination of the interests of the national capitalists. Its power should be supported by the Social-Democratic Parties participating in its deliberations, in order to support a policy of peace in their "own" countries.

The demand for general disarmament and free trade should follow logically from such an attitude. But on these questions the ideas of the various social-democratic parties are sharply divided, reflecting the hostile interests of the national bourgeoisie.

On the military question: the German social-democracy is opposed to the militia and supports the National Guard (Reichswehr).

"Our attitude to the Reichswehr cannot be one of opposition in principle; the Reichswehr is in its very nature a system of defence with which we can agree in the circumstances provided that disarmament, which is nowadays one-sided, does not become international.... We do not therefore struggle against the Reichswehr, but for it, so as to make it a still more reliable instrument in the hands of the republic." (Hilferding at Kiel.)

On the other hand, the French social-democracy whose member, Paul Boncour, is well known as the protagonist of the new French military system, announces the necessity of a general obligation to serve—extended even to women—and the subordination of all the economic forces of the country to the purposes of "national defence."

The social-democrats of the small countries whose capitalists cannot conduct any independent policy, such as the Swiss, Norwegian, Dutch, Swedish and Danish Social Democratic Parties, are all in favour of complete or very extensive disarmament.

The attitude of the various Social-Democratic Parties to the question of tariffs is equally contradictory.

We wish to emphasise again that this outline portrayal of the reformists of today is not applicable everywhere, for there is no definite international theory, just as there is no international discipline, among the reformists. But our statement represents the kernel of social-democratic ideas. The central point of their theory is the theory of the State set up in opposition to that of Marx. If the State today is considered not as a tool of the capitalist class, but as an instrument which can be employed, according to the election result, as the tool of one class or another, including the working class, then everything else follows logically from that: the importance of parliamentary democracy, the Utopia of achieving economic democracy by means of the ballot box, the possibility of a peaceful transition from capitalism to socialism—if only the ruling class will respect democracy. The theory that there is no room for Communism also follows from this.[3]

It is unnecessary to refute these social-democratic theories in these pages. Experience refutes them from first to last. Capitalist terror is ruling instead of democracy over an ever larger area. The capitalists prove at every moment that the State today is a bourgeois State, and they only put up with democracy as long as it does not endanger their class supremacy.

But the reformists are not particularly concerned as to whether their theories are true or false. For them, as capitalist agents in the working class, it is enough if large sections of workers believe in the correctness of their theories. They themselves surrender these theories as soon as they involve any danger to their "own" bourgeoisie. They support the maintenance of imperialist power where the capitalists possess such power (MacDonald); they are in favour of the re-division of the world if their "own" bourgeoisie feels itself wronged (Labriola); in the victorious countries they support the maintenance of the status quo arrived at after the war; in the defeated countries they favour a revision of the peace treaty; they compromise with the Fascists (Polish Socialist Party) and continuously incite hatred against the U.S.S.R. Sometimes they are in opposition, sometimes in office, but even when in opposition they are always the future Government Party, the party for the defence of the capitalist system. If they are in opposition they carry on trade union struggles which, viewed historically, only serve the purpose of retaining the confidence of the working class in order to be able to proceed more strongly and more effectively against revolution when any new and acutely revolutionary situation arises.

The problem is: how can the reformists, with such contradictory theories, hostile to the interests of the working class, daily refuted by practical experience, how can they keep such great masses of workers under their banner? It would overstep the limits of our work if we were to give a full answer to this question: we should merely like to mention a few points. The labour aristocracy, that section of the working class corrupted by the capitalists, belong by their very nature and class position, to the reformists. The reformists also attract those sections of the proletariat which do not possess the necessary resolution and fighting spirit to join the Communists, but for whom activity in the social-democratic party gives the illusion of struggle against capitalism. The reformists also include those wide sections of the working class which not so very long ago were part of the peasantry and of the middle classes, and who still drag with them the idea of an expansion within capitalism, etc. The more acutely the inherent contradictions of capitalism develop, the more the supremacy of monopoly capital comes to be felt, the quicker will social democracy lose its influence over the workers, as the recent successes of the German, French and English Communist Parties show. Hilferding's contention that the Communist Party is lost, is actually applicable to the Social Democratic Party as a party of the working class. Its character of a bourgeois party is being more extensively recognised by the proletariat, and all those who are courageous, youthful and eager for the fight, are leaving the ranks of social democracy.

NOTES

1. In the form of an attack on the theory of passively awaiting the collapse of capitalism, supposed to be propagated by the Communists; the theory emphasised by us, of the necessity for the violent overthrow of capitalism by the proletarian revolution, is ignored, and the purest revisionism is announced as Marxism. For example, Otto Braunthal writes as follows in his booklet destined for the socialist youth: "Tendencies in the Development of Capitalist Economy":

   "Diametrically opposed to the theory of collapse, the theory of concentration is a soundly optimistic theory of development. It believes that the development of capitalist economy—apart from temporary retrogressions—will continue until its transformation into socialism. It also believes that it is possible for the workers to gain a share in the continually increasing production by means of rises in real wages, in spite of the falling value of labour power. And, in conclusion, it considerably lightens the tasks of the socialist transformation by assuming that the organisation of economic life is possible and sensible, step by step. Two advantages of socialist society can be inferred from this conception. Firstly, all tendencies in organisation, which nowadays are penetrating all the nooks and corners of capitalist economy, will become preparations for fulfilling the tasks of socialist organisation. Secondly, the socialist society is not faced with the insoluble problem of changing an anarchic economy into an organised economy by one stroke; but it is faced with the much easier task of gradually changing a semi-organised economic life into a fully organised one."

2. This is the demand of all trade unionists from Green (U.S.A.) to Jouhaux (France).
3. Hilferding said at Kiel: "The Communists are disappearing, although it may take a longer or shorter time. I can understand that the unemployed, the many desperate persons who lost their money during inflation, that all those who, during the war, lost everything but their belief in force, still perhaps, from some blind instinct vote for the Communists. But the Communist Party is of no importance in the socialist movement. It is lost."

12

Conclusion

The work of Communists is more difficult and complicated now than it was a few years ago. Stabilisation of capitalism means that there is no acutely revolutionary situation in the great capitalist countries. Communists must accomplish the task of working between two waves of revolution as a revolutionary mass party, or of creating such a party. They must be the vanguard, steadfastly working towards the revolutionary goal, but not, in so doing, allowing themselves to be separated from the workers, not becoming an isolated sect. They must be mass parties; this means that the daily interests of the working masses, of all the exploited, must be defended; and the bourgeoisie fought consistently and logically even within the framework of capitalism.

In this sphere, the Communists and the reformists are in keen competition for the masses. With stabilisation, the position of the reformists has to a certain extent improved. Wide sections of the working class, temporarily discouraged by many defeats in the revolutionary struggle, believe their promises, that capitalism has entered a new period of expansion, in which the workers will also have their share. The rise in real wages in a few countries in recent years gave some foundation for these hopes. The fact that the reformist trade unions are again conducting separate industrial struggles—at the moment there is no danger of every working class struggle changing into a revolutionary struggle for power—assists the reformists to gain adherents among the masses. All these factors intensify the difficulties of our task in capitalist countries.

But the change in already in progress. The working class is beginning to realise that capitalist rationalisation is not a universal panacea. Mass unemployment is increasing. The last results in Germany and France show a further growth in the influence of the Communist Party, although the social-democrats also succeeded in increasing the number of their voters. In England, the Communist Party is on the road to becoming a mass party.

Appendix

CHAPTER 1

Table I

This includes only the most important raw materials, for there are no international statistics for manufactured goods. We may, however, assume that the production of finished goods runs in general parallel to that of raw materials, that in fact, it oversteps raw materials a little, for one of the most important methods of reducing costs of production is the better utilisation of raw materials and the avoidance of waste.

The table shows that the production of all raw materials is greater than before the war, but that the increase in those raw materials which are included in Division I of Marx's scheme—particularly metals—is much greater than in foodstuffs and textiles. This indicates the great expansion in the machinery of production, and consequently the strong tendency towards accumulation and concentration. Increases in the production of foodstuffs and textile materials just keep pace with the growth of population, which shows that the population's standard of life has not improved—that of the workers certainly not.

The figures are not very reliable (particularly those referring to agriculture), but are adequate for general inference.

The Most Important Figures of Production of World Economy (I)

			Yearly Average 1909-13	*Yearly Average 1920-24*	*1925*	*1926*	*1927*
				In Million Units			
Food							
Wheat (1)	Area	ha.*	79.8	83.3	89.6	91.8	–
	Produce	tons	82.2	88.7	90.2	91.8	94.7
Rye (1)	Area	ha.	19.6	18.3	18.7	18.2	–
	Produce	tons	26.1	21.1	25.6	20.4	23.1
Barley(1)	Area	ha.	23.6	24.5	25.5	25.5	–
	Produce	tons	28.7	27.6	30.9	29.5	30.9
Oats(1)	Area	ha.	41.1	44.2	45.6	44.1	–
	Produce	tons	52.1	52.0	58.2	53.8	53.6
Maize (1)	Area	ha.	69.9	70.2	71.7	70.0	–
	Produce	tons	102.9	108.0	113.6	107.0	–
Rice	Area	ha.	48.2	53.6(3)	54.7	54.3	–
	Produce	tons	77.5	83.2(3)	85.3	84.6	–
Potatoes (1)	Area	ha.	12.4	12.5	12.4	12.7	–
	Produce	tons	128.6	128.8	143.6	120.9	145.5
Beet Sugar (1)	Produce	doz.	69.7	57.0	73.2	69.1	73.6
Cane Sugar (1)	Produce	doz.	96.0	139.0	166.0	159.2	157.3
Textiles							
Cotton	Production	tons	4.84	4.33	6.0	5.99	4.40
	Consumption	bales	23.3 (3)	21.6	23.2 (5)	24.7 (4)	25.9

Wool	Production	kg.	1463.0	1249.0(6)	1329.0	1405.0	–
Silk	Production	kg.	29.2	38.2	45.8	47.2	–
Artificial Silk	Production	kg.	14.1(2)	49.4(6)	87.0	99.5	130.0
Rubber	Production	kg.	114.0 (2)	303.0	504.0	618.0	604.0
Fuel							
Coal	Production	tons	1098.0	1126.0	1187.0	1217.0	1283.0
Petroleum	Production	barrels	385.0	869.0	1067.0	1095.0	1234.0
Metals							
Iron	Production	tons	68.3	58.9	76.9	77.5	85.0
Steel	Production	tons	65.2	68.4	90.8	91.6	99.1
Copper	Production	kg.	1030.0(2)	1015.0	1443.0	1491.0	1510.0
Lead	Production	kg.	1194.0(2)	1084.0	1524.0	1587.0	1643.0
Zinc	Production	kg.	976.0(2)	760.0	1132.0	1249.0	1300.0
Tin	Production	kg.	133.0(2)	128.0	150.0	147.0	–
Aluminium	Production	kg.	63.0(2)	122.0	179.0	211.0	213.0
Gold	Production	1000 kg.	768.0(2)	525.0	593.0	600.0	600.0
Silver	Production	1000 kg.	6964.0(2)	6467.0	7514.0	7454.0	7454.0
Shipbuilding Launched from							
Docks	1000 British	tons	3333.0(2)	3312.0	2193.0	1675.0	2236.0

(1) Source of figures: International Statistical Year Book, 1926. International Handbook of Agricultural Statistics. 1926-27. For 1927 (and partly 1923) newspapers and other publications.
(1) Excluding the Soviet Union. (2) 1913. (3) 1912-13. (4) 1925-26 (5) 1924-25 (6) 1922-24 (7) Current figures. (8) 1926-27.
* 1 hectare equals 2 ½ acres.

Table Ia

World Population (1)

	1913	*1926*	*Percentage Increase over 1913*
	In Millions		
Europe	467.9	477.6	2.1
North and Central America	133.5	157.5	17.9
South America	56.5	69.7	23.5
Asia	986.7	1037.9	5.2
Africa	134.2	143.3	6.8
Oceana	7.7	9.0	17.8
	1786.5	1895.0	6.1

(1) International Agricultural Statistical Annual, Rome, 1926-27.

Table II

Table II shows the development in production and consumption of the most important raw materials in Europe. It can be seen the production of foodstuffs in Europe (excluding the Soviet Union), as well as the consumption of cotton and wool, was, even in 1927, below the pre-war average, although population has increased since then.

European Figures of Production (1)

			Yearly Average 1909-13	*Yearly Average 1920-24*	*1925*	*1926*	*1927*
			In Million Units				
Foodstuffs							
Wheat (1)	Area	ha.	29.3	26.7	27.8	27.9	28.4
	Produce	tons	37.1	30.5	37.8	33.0	34.6
Rye(1)	Area	ha.	18.2	15.4	16.4	16.2	16.3
	Produce	tons	25.1	18.6	23.8	19.0	21.1
Barley(1)	Area	ha.	11.5	10.8	11.1	11.0	11.2
	Produce	tons	15.4	13.5	15.1	15.0	14.6
Oats(1)	Area	ha.	20.0	18.4	18.7	18.7	18.5
	Produce	tons	28.2	23.5	26.0	27.8	27.1
Maize (1)	Area	ha.	10.9	9.9	10.9	10.8	11.4
	Produce	tons	16.0	11.6	15.9	16.9	12.2
Rice (1)	Area	ha.	0.2	0.18	0.2	0.2	–
	Produce	tons	0.7	0.8	1.0	1.0	–
Potatoes (1)	Area	ha.	10.5	10.1	10.4	10.3	10.6
	Produce	tons	114.0	111.0	129.4	104.4	127.0

Beet Sugar (1)	Produce	doz.	52.9	46.0	64.2	59.2	64.1
Textiles							
Cotton	Consumption	bales	12.2(3)	8.3	9.8(3)	10.2(4)	10.3(8)
Wool	Production	kg.	431.0	326.0(6)	331.0	340.0	–
Silk	Production	kg.	4.7	3.8	4.7	4.2	–
Artificial Silk	Production	kg.	13.4(2)	34.6(6)	56.9	63.3	93.0
Fuel							
Coal	Production	tons	552.0	491.0	545.0	463.0	610.0
Petroleum	Production	barrels	85.0	51.0	76.0	93.0	104.0
Metals							
Iron	Production	tons	39.2	25.5	37.0	35.1	44.9
Steel	Production	tons	36.0	29.5	40.8	40.5	51.5
Copper	Production	kg.	192.0(2)	86.0	106.0	125.0	–
Lead	Production	kg.	559.0(2)	263.0	371.0	345.0	–
Zinc	Production	kg.	647.0(2)	326.0	514.0	528.0	618.0
Tin	Production	kg.	37.0(2)	30.0	42.0	–	–
Aluminium	Production	kg.	37.0(2)	63.0	104.0	103.0	–
Silver	Production	1000 kg.	474.0(2)	266.0	327.0	338.0	–
Shipbuilding	Launched from						
Docks	1000 British	tons	2914.0(2)	2427.0	2030.0	1428.0	–

(1) Source of figures: International Statistical Year Book, 1926. International Book of Agricultural Statistics. 1926-27. For 1927 (and partly 1926) newspapers and other publications.

(1) Excluding the Soviet Union. (2) 1913. (3) 1912-13. (4) 1925-26 (5) 1924-25 (6) 1922-24 (7) Current figures. (8) 1926-27.

Table IIa

Europe–America

This table shows that Europe's share in heavy industry production has increased in recent years, while that of America has fallen relatively; development is approaching the conditions of the pre-war period. In the textile industry the development is similar, but much more slow. In considering the figures, the bad markets for the United States in 1927, and the good markets for Germany in that year must not be left out of account.

Percentage Comparison of Europeans and American Shares in World Production

	EUROPE			*UNITED STATES*		
	1909-13	*1920-24*	*1927*	*1909-13*	*1920-24*	*1927*
Coal	50.4	43.6	50.2	42.5	55.7	42.4
Iron	57.3	43.3	53.0	39.8	52.6	43.6
Steel	55.2	43.1	52.1	42.5	53.6	47.2
Cotton Consumption	52.5	38.4	40.0	24.0	27.9	27.4

Diagram I

From the "Literary Digest," March 24, 1928.

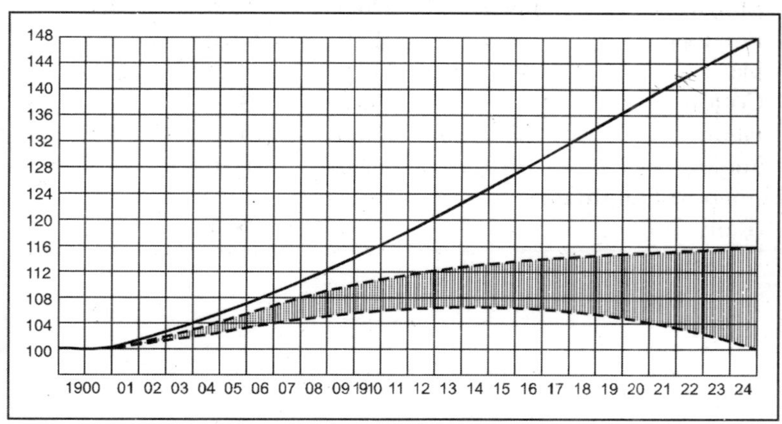

1. Development of agricultural production in U.S.A. since 1899.
2. Growth of agricultural population.
3. Number of workers employed in agriculture.
4. Grey shaded area shows number of workers unemployed in agriculture.

Chapter II
Table III

Index Figures of the Economy of the Soviet Union
(Taken from the Russian Control Figures for 1927-28.)

	1924-25	*1925-26*	*1926-27*	*1927-28*
Industry				
Coal	55.3	84.1	107.2	124.1
Petroleum	76.1	89.8	109.7	120.7
Pig Iron	30.6	52.4	70.5	82.3
Metals	39.6	64.1	76.3	85.2
Cotton Yarn	67.0	90.6	105.4	112.0
Rubber Shoes	56.4	90.7	109.6	132.6
Salt	68.2	80.3	102.0	114.2
Agriculture				
Cultivated Area	84.4	89.4	95.1	97.6
Cattle	–	–	96.9	102.8
Wheat	81.0	94.0	108.0	104.0
Rye	108.0	109.0	120.0	127.0
Barley	41.0	65.0	63.0	57.0
Oats	51.0	76.0	105.0	94.0
Maize	149.0	376.0	277.0	278.0
Potatoes	–	219.0	245.0	–
Flax	91.0	110.0	97.0	121.0
Cotton	–	56.0	56.0	–
Hemp	83.0	150.0	134.0	148.0
Sugar	30.0	67.0	60.0	–
Transport Freightage				
(Railways)	–	–	99.1	114.2

Table IV

Development of Production in the U.S.S.R. and the Rest of Europe

The League of Nations has issued the following index figure of production, based on the production of 63 raw products (foods, fibrous materials, metals, fuel, chemicals) calculated on 1926 prices.

	1913	*1923*	*1924*	*1925*	*1926*
Europe, excluding U.S.S.R.	100	87	93	102	93
Europe, including U.S.S.R.	100	84	89	102	98

The figures show that in 1926 the production of the U.S.S.R. outstripped that of the rest of Europe.

CHAPTER II
Tables V and VI

The tables show the great increase of German production in the last few years in every sphere. Although it does not reach the rate of development of industrial production in the Soviet Union, it is still the only example in economic history. It must, however, be taken into account that structural and market factors coincided favourably. It is possible that after the end of the rationalisation market a decrease in the volume of production will set in.

Table V

Production in Germany (1)

		1913	*1920*	*1924*	*1925*	*1926*	*1927*
Coal	Million tons	141.0	108.0	119.0	132.0	145.0	154.0
Brown Coal	" "	87.0	112.0	125.0	140.0	139.0	151.0
Coke	" "	35.0	26.0	25.0	28.0	26.0	32.0
Pig Iron	" "	10.9	6.4	7.8	10.1	9.6	13.1
Raw Steel	" "	11.7	8.4	9.7	12.1	12.3	16.3
Potash	" "	11.6	11.4	8.1	12.1	9.4	–
Cotton Consumption	1000 tons	486.0(2)	163.0	271.0	368.0	292.0	475.0
Shipbuilding Launched from Docks	1000 tons	465.0(2)	242.0	175.0	406.0	180.0	290.0

(1) German Statistical Year Book, 1927. (2) Old sphere of territory.

Table VI

Index Figures of German Production (1)

		Total	*Industries Handling Raw Materials*	*Manufacturing Industries*
1924		1924-25 = 100.		
1.	Quarter	77.5	73.0	88.2
2.	"	86.1	81.0	98.0
3.	"	86.1	88.3	81.0
4.	"	101.6	101.4	102.5
1925.				
1.	Quarter	111.8	112.0	111.6
2.	"	107.1	107.3	106.8
3.	"	103.3	100.4	110.0
4.	"	104.1	100.3	112.8
1926.				
1.	Quarter	94.4	95.0	93.3
2.	"	91.4	95.6	82.1
3.	"	100.7	105.0	91.0
4.	"	116.7	118.5	112.6
1927.				
1.	Quarter	121.9	122.7	120.3
2.	"	122.5	122.0	123.8
3.	"	123.3	122.2	125.9

(1) Quarterly Market Reports

Chapter II

Table VII

Production in France

Figures of French production show a much slower increase than those for Germany. The stabilisation crisis is reflected in the stagnation of production for the year 1927.

		1913	*1920*	*1924*	*1925*	*1926*	*1927*
Coal	Million tons	44.0	25.0	45.0	48.0	52.0	52.0
Pig Iron	" "	9.0	3.3	7.7	8.5	9.4	9.3
Raw Steel	" "	7.0	2.7	6.9	7.4	8.4	8.2
Potash	" "	–	1.2	1.7	1.9	2.3	–
Cotton Consumption	1000 bales	1010.0	–	1063.0	1122.0	1179.0	1182.0
Shipbuilding. Launched from Docks	1000 tons	176.0	93.0	80.0	76.0	121.0	44.0

Table VIII

Production in England(1)

English production statistics show stagnation in the great staple industries, among which only the production of steel exceeds that of the pre-war period; while all others have not yet reached that figure. The figures also show the upward movement in the new industries.

		1913	*1920*	*1924*	*1925*	*1926*	*1927*
Coal	Million tons	287.0	233.0	270.0	247.0	131.0	259.0
Iron	" "	10.3	8.2	7.3	6.2	2.4	7.3
Steel	" "	7.7	9.2	8.2	7.7	3.6	9.1
Shipbuilding	1000 tons	1932.0	2056.0	1440.0	1079.0	640.0	1226.0
Electrical	(1929 = 100)	—	100.0	—	76.0	87.0	114.0
Motors	(in thousand)	22.0(1)	-	132.0	176.0	159.0	200.0
Cotton Consumption	(1000 bales)	3825.0	-	2718.0	3235.0	3022/0	3010.0

(1) *The Economist*, 11.2.28. (1) 1912.

Chapter II Table IX

Production in the United States(1)

American production statistics show a more or less uniform rise up to 1926, and a fairly heavy decline in all important industries in 1927.

		1913	*1920*	*1924*	*1925*	*1926*	*1927*(9)
Coal (2)	Million short tons	478	569	494	520	578	520
Anthracite	" " "	91	90	88	62	85	81
Coke	" " "	46	51	44	51	56	50
Petroleum	" barrels	248	463	714	764	767	890
Iron	" long tons	31	37	31	37	39	36
Steel	" " "	31	42	38	45	48	43
Copper	1000 short tons	807	763	1130	1102	1173	-
Lead	" " "	462	530	690	767	799	-
Zinc	" " "	347	463	517	573	618	-
Automobiles(1)	1000's	462	1883	3243	3839	3937	2939
Tractors	"	24	322	364	473	491	455
Cotton Consumption	1000 bales	5786	6762	5522	6433	6687	7406
Building(4)	Million dollars	858	2533	3880	5043	5391	-
Value added in Industry	Milliards	9.7(6)	24.7(7)	-	26.8	-	-
Wholesale Trade Index	-	100	226(8)	150	159	151	147

(1) Statistical Abstract of the U.S.A., and Commerce Year Book, 1926. (2) Bituminous. (3) Motors for private use in U.S.A. and Canada. (4) In 27 States. (5) 1914.(6) 1919. (7) 1919-206. (8) Survey of Current Business.

Diagram II

From the "Literary Digest," March 24, 1928.

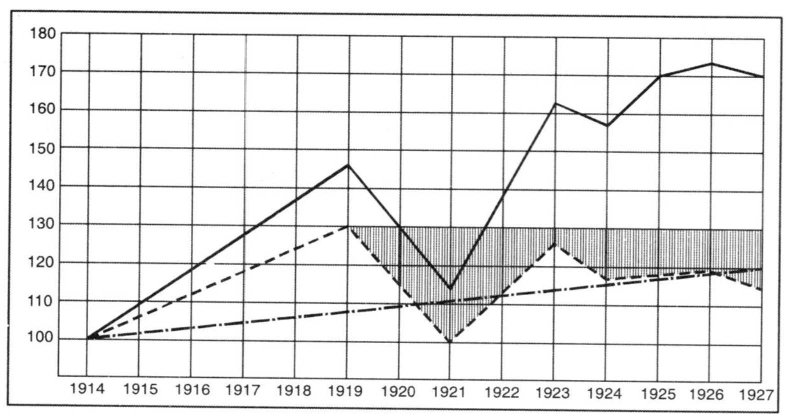

1. Large-scale industry production in U.S.A.
2. Number of workers employed in large-scale industry.
3. Changes in population.
4. The grey shaded part shows the number of workers unemployed in production since 1919.

Chapter III

Table X

Unemployment

The following figures do not give a complete picture of unemployment, but only of those officially registered as unemployed, which is considerably lower. For England, figures relating to young workers who have not yet found employment are lacking: for Germany, those relating to persons on poor law and those run out of benefit. The statistics, therefore, can only give a dynamic picture. As such, they demonstrate the *permanent character of mass unemployment in the period of stabilisation.*

Number of Unemployed Officially Registered. In Thousands

	England	*Germany*	*Italy*	*Poland*	*Belgium*	*Austria*	*Czecho-slovakia*	*Holland*	*Switzer-land*
4th Quarter, 1920	526	368	104	–	49	16	20	33	15
July, 1921	1804	314	414	65	147	–	33	30	56
Dec. 1921	1934	149	542	173	36	–	33	66	89
July, 1922	1458	20	372	87	36	38(1)	232(1)	33	52
Dec. 1922	1432	43	382	75	26	117	437	50	53
July, 1923	1325	139(2)	183	65	14	87	215	31	23
Dec. 1923	1227	1528(2)	259	68	24	98	192	45	27
July, 1924	1135	526	118	152	21	66	63	19	8
Dec. 1924	1260	536	150	159	33	154	81	35	11
July, 1925	1327	197	80	175	31	112	42	23	10
Dec. 1925	1243	1498	112	314	44	179	43	45	17
July, 1926	1737	1741	80	263	16	152	46	20	11
Dec. 1926	1432	1749	192	190	33	205	29	36	18
July, 1927	1114	573	388	148	22	137	12	21	8
Dec. 1927	1194	1188	414	165	56	207	–	–	14

(1) September. (2) Unoccupied territory only.

Percentage of Trade Union Unemployed, or of Unemployed Insured Workers

	Holland	*Denmark*	*Sweden*	*Norway*	*Germany*	*England*	*Canada*	*U.S.A.*
4th Quarter, 1920	8.3	8.3	9.3	3.9	4.1	4.5	9.3	–
July, 1921	7.6	16.7	27.8	17.9	2.6	14.8	9.1	–
Dec. 1921	16.6	25.2	33.2	18.3	1.6	16.2	15.1	–
July, 1922	9.1	13.2	21.5	15.6	0.6	15.7	5.3	–
Dec. 1922	15.1	20.3	21.3	15.1	2.8	14.0	6.1	–
July, 1923	10.6	7.5	9.1	6.9	3.5	11.5	2.2	–
Dec. 1923	15.9	19.6	14.1	14.0	28.2	10.7	7.2	–
July, 1924	7.0	5.4	6.2	3.9	12.5	9.9	5.4	–
Dec. 1924	12.7	17.1	15.5	12.5	8.1	10.0	11.6	–
July, 1925	8.3	8.3	7.6	8.3	3.7	11.2	5.2	–
Dec. 1925	16.0	31.1	19.4	19.0	19.4	10.5	7.9	–
July, 1926	6.9	17.0	8.6	20.4	17.7	14.0	2.3	–
Dec. 1926	12.1	32.2	19.1	29.6	16.7	11.9	5.9	–
July, 1927	7.0	17.3	8.2	20.9	5.5	9.3	3.3	–
Dec. 1927	9.3	30.5	18.6	28.0	12.9	9.8	6.6	17.8

Chapter III

Table XI

Increases of Output in Germany

Exact statistics of output and production are not available for Germany as for the U.S.A. The following data make it reasonable to assume that mass unemployment is developing in Germany also. The number of workers in those concerns employing more than five workers, which come into the scope of industrial statistics, amounted.

in thousands, to(1)—

	1922	1924	1925	1926	1927
	8216	7386	–	6920	–
National Statistical Dept. Index of Production. 1924-26 = 100	–	100	101	111	125

The index of production is based on a relatively small number of commodities (2), and has only a roughly approximate value. But the following figures for separate industries confirm this tendency to a great increase in labour output, although one cannot judge from them how much is due to increased productivity, and how much to increased intensity. The figures are taken from the Annual Report of the National Credit Company.

	1925		End 1927
1. Ruhr Coal Mining: Increasing in production per shift from	114	to	132
2. Pig Iron Production: Daily output per worker increased from	100	to	140
3. Raw Steel Production: Daily output per worker increased from	100	to	137
	Ist Quarter, 1925.		3rd Quarter, 1927.
4. Machine Industry: from	100	to	145
	1925		1927
5. National Railways: Km. per head of personnel from	100	to	118.5

(1) Figures for 1922 and 1924 from 1926 Statistical Year Book; 1926 from Annual Report of the Industrial Department. The Report contains no figures for metals, building, etc, which are included in the 1924 figures. Judging from the tendency towards a decrease in all industries, this, if

anything, makes the figures rather than lower.

(2) See Quarterly Market Reports for 1927.

Chapter IV

Calculation of the Rate of Surplus Value in American Industry

The statistics collected by the Census, which is taken periodically afford the possibility of making an approximate estimate of the rate of surplus value in American industry. The factors entering into such a calculation are (see Commerce Year Book, 1926):—

Total wages	=	Variable capital
Cost of raw materials	=	Circulating capital
Cost of wear and tear of machinery	=	Fixed capital
The value of the product.		

For an exact calculation we should also have—

1. The value of the wear and tear of that part of the fixed capital present in buildings; but this is relatively so small that it can be overlooked in any merely approximate calculation.

2. There is also lacking a very important factor, namely the total of commercial profits, which is a part of the surplus value produced in industry, for in the Marxian theory of value industrial capital disposes of its goods to commercial capital not at the full production price, but lower than that, at a price which will enable commercial capital, when selling the commodities at their production price, to realise the average rate of profit. Profit on commercial capital is therefore surplus value produced in industry, and if we are to find the actual rate of surplus value, it must be added to the surplus value shown in industry. The necessary data are not, however, at our disposal. Consequently the rate of surplus value in the next table is considerably lower than corresponds to reality.

With these reservation let us turn to the tables:—

	Total Wages = V	*Cost of Materials = C*	*Wear and Tear of Machinery = fixed C*	*Value Produced*	*Total Surplus Value = S*	*Rate of Surplus Value %*
	I	*II*	*III*	*IV*	*V*	*VI*
			In Million Dollars		$\text{IV} - (\text{I} + \text{II} + \text{III})$	$\frac{\text{V}}{\text{I}} = \frac{\text{S}}{\text{V}}$
1889	2,008	6,576	250	11,407	2,569	123
1904	2,610	8,500	330	14,494	3,354	128
1909	3,427	12,143	500	20,672	4,602	134
1914	4,068	14,278	600	23,988	5,042	121
1919	10,453	36,989	1,600	61,737	12,695	121
1921	8,193	25,155	1,400	43,427	8,679	105
1923	10,999	34,381	1,800	60,258	12,978	117
1925	10,729	35,931	2,300	62,706	13,746	128

For calculating the wear and tear of machines the figures giving the total value of machines employed in industry are at our disposal (taken from the Official Publication, "Wealth, Public Debt and Taxation, 1922," p. 18.):—

In Million Dollars

1900	*1904*	*1912*	*1922*
2541	3298	6091	15,783

If we consider this table the most important thing we learn from it is that the 100 per cent rate of surplus value assumed by Marx and everywhere described as grossly exaggerated, has actually been outstripped in American industry. And we must again emphasise the fact that this rate of surplus value is lower than the actual rate, for it does not include that share of the profits produced in industry, but going to commercial capital.

We wish to emphasise, moreover, very strongly that we are *dealing here only with a very rough attempt at estimating the approximate rate of surplus value, based on inadequate data and with many deviations from the actual facts,* but at least these deviations tend to make the result lower than the actual rate of surplus value.

Chapter VI

Table XV

Capital Issues and Movements of Capital

The following table shows capital export of the two principal countries, U.S.A. and England, in recent years, and German capital import. We must point out: 1.—that we are only daling with public issues, 2. —that apart from long -term capital export from the U.S.A. and England, there is also a stream of short-term investment capital to these countries.

New Issues and Capital Export, England

In million £ (i)

	1912	*1913*	*1924*	*1925*	*1926*	*1927*
England.						
Government	—	—	13.8	45.7	4.7	66.1
Other	45.3	36.0	70.8	109.3	124.5	140.8
	45.2	36.0	84.6	155.0	129.2	206.9
British Possessions						
Government	14.7	26.3	50.1	30.7	31.9	55.7
Other	58.0	49.9	22.2	30.2	21.3	44.1
	72.7	76.2	72.3	60.9	53.2	99.8
Foreign						
Government	9.6	26.2	40.6	—	23.8	11.8
Other	83.3	58.3	11.8	16.3	24.6	36.6
	92.9	84.5	52.4	16.3	48.4	48.4
Total	210.9	196.7	209.3	232.2	230.8	355.1

The table does not include any conversion operations, but represents exclusively new capital

New Issues and Capital Export, United States.
Issued in million dollars. (1)

	Total	*Aborad*
1923	4,304	267
1924	5,593	997
1925	6,223	1,086
1926	6,311	1,145
1927	—	1,567

New Issues and Capital Import, Germany (2)

	Internal Loan	Actual Foreign Loans	Joint Stock Amounts Raised	Capital Demand
		In Million Marks		
1924 total	176.30	1,002.00	66.00	113.88
1925	144.60	1241.00	593.76	114.12
1926	1306.00	1517.00	1242.66	90.38
1927	993.70	1688.38	1024.13	139.90

(*i*) "Information Financier," 1/12/27.
(1) "Commercial and Financial Chronicle."
(2) "Frankfurter Zeitung," 1/1/28.

Chapter VI

Table XVI

Comparative Index Figures of Real Wages (1)

The following table gives a very rough sketch of real wages in the period of stabilisation in the most important European capitals. They are comparable with each other only with many reservations, for the *method of calculation* varies greatly from town to town.

Calculated on the basis of food prices, London 1 VII, 24 = 100.

	1924 Ist July	*1927 Ist October*
Amsterdam	89	86
Berlin	55	68
Brussels	59	50
London	100	105
Madrid	57	57
Rome	46	51
Paris	73	56(3)
Prague	56	52
Vienna	47	45
Warsaw	43(2)	42
Lodz	48(2)	44

(1) International Labour Review, October, 1927. The figures of the I. L.O. can be used to determine the tendency in wage developments.
(2) 1st January, 1925.
(3) 1st July, 1927.

Chapter VI

Table XVII

Wage Changes in Germany, 1913-1927

This table is taken or calculated from official statistics. In these statistics wages for full-time workers under agreements are given as for the highest paid section; on the other hand, the official cost of living index is too low; in particular, the deductions for taxation and social purposes, much higher than before the war, are not taken into consideration.

	Weekly Skilled	*Wages in Marks Unskilled*	*Real Wage Skilled*	*Index Unskilled*
1913	35.02	24.31	100	100
February, 1924	28.61	22.86	72	94
December, 1924	38.44	28.61	83	90
February, 1925	39.18	29.23	81	89
July, 1925	43.90	32.37	87	93
December, 1925	45.98	33.92	93	99
February, 1926	46.02	33.95	94	100
July, 1926	45.93	34.05	92	99
December, 1926	46.36	34.44	92	98
February, 1927	46.43	34.52	91	98
July, 1927	49.17	36.70	93	100
December, 1927	49.43	37.01	93	101

Chapter VI

Table XVIII

Wage Changes in England

The following table of wage changes in England does not take into account the cheapening in cost of living following upon deflation. It *cannot*, therefore, be used as a basis for determining real wages:—

	Increase In Total Weekly Wages	*Decrease Bill, £1,000*
1915	867	–
1916	885	–
1917	2986	–
1918	3435	–
1919	2547	–
1920	4793	–
1921	–	6061
1922	–	4210

1923	–	317
1924	554	–
1925	–	78
1926	49	–
1927	–	359
	16.116	11.025

Chapter VI

Table XIX

Wages in the U.S.A.
Real Wage Index in the U.S.A. (1)

Yearly	Average	1912	100
"	"	1923	103
"	"	1924	111
"	"	1925	107
"	"	1926	110
"	"	1927	112 (2)

(1) "American Federationist," December, 1927. This index figure is calculated on the basis of the prices of goods consumed by the workers.

(2) Average for first 9 months.

Real Wages, Index Nos. According to Official Statistics

			Total Wage Index for Industrial Workers	*Department of Labour Cost of Living Index*	*Real Wage Index*
1914	Monthly	average	100.0	100	100
1920	"	"	235.4	198	119
1921	"	"	188.0	167	113
1922	"	"	191.9	157	122
1923	"	"	211.3	161	131
1924	"	"	209.5	164	128
1925	"	"	214.8	168	128
1926	"	"	216.7	168	128
1927	April	"	218.4	164	133

In the four years 1924-27 real wages changed on the average very little in the U.S.A. *Since the 4th Quarter of 1927 wage decreases have set in.*

Chapter VI

Table XX

Consumption Per Head of Articles of General Consumption in Germany (1)

The table shows that consumption per head of the population, corresponding to the impoverishment of broad masses, is still lower than before the war.

		1913(2) (1913-1914)	*1923 (1922-1923)*	*1924 (1923-1924)*	*1925 (1924-1925)*	*1926 (1925-1926)*	*1927(3) (1926-1927)*
Rye	kg.	153	90	106	87	115	101
Wheat	kg.	96	47	57	68	74	80
Barley	kg.	108	29	42	45	58	66
Oats	kg.	128	57	87	85	86	106
Potatoes	kg.	700	560	433	495	582	478
Meat	kg.	52	31	43	47	48	–
Beer	litre	102	45	61	75	76	–
Spirits	litre	5.4	2.5	1.88	2.8	3.0	–
Sugar	kg.	19.0	19.5	13.3	20.2	20.5	–
Coffee	kg.	2.4	0.6	0.9	1.4	1.7	1.9
Cotton	kg.	7.2	3.0	4.3	5.9	4.7	7.5

(1) Statistical Year Book for Germany, 1927.
(2) Old extent of territory.
(3) Current figures.

Chapter VI

Table XXI

British Imports Per Head of the Most Important Foodstuffs, etc. (3)

The import of the most important foodstuffs, etc., into England is greater than before the war, which can be attributed to the increased purchasing power of the masses following on deflation.

		1913(1)	*1923(1)*	*1924(1)*	*1925(2)*	*1926(2)*	*1927(2)*
Wheat	lbs.	259.0	247.0	291.0	239.0	240.0	272.0
Flour	"	29.0	29.0	27.0	22.0	26.0	27.0
Maize	"	118.0	82.0	91.0	65.0	79.0	112.0
Beef	"	22.0	30.6	30.4	30.2	32.7	32.3
Mutton	"	13.0	14.5	12.8	13.4	13.3	13.7
Ham and Bacon	"	13.7	22.6	22.3	21.3	20.5	22.3

Butter	"	9.9	12.2	12.7	13.3	13.9	13.8
Cheese	"	5.5	6.9	7.1	7.3	7.4	7.2
Sugar	"	82.4	71.7	76.9	106.3	88.3	81.7
Tea	"	6.7	8.5	8.8	9.0	9.2	10.1
Tobacco	"	2.06	2.3	2.85	3.97	4.16	4.70
Eggs	No.	56.2	52.89	53.5	–	55.1	60.6
Wine	gallons	0.25	0.30	0.34	–	0.43	0.44

(1) Statistical Abstract for the United Kingdom.
(2) Calculated by the Author on figures published in Board of Trade Journal.
(3) Including Northern Ireland.

Of the foodstuffs included in the table above, there is also produced at home:—

Percentage of Total Consumption.

Meat	*Eggs*	*Wheat*	*Cheese*	*Butter*	*Sugar*	*Bacon*
43	38	28	15	10	10	7

Chapter IX

Table XXII

Industrialisation

Coal Production in 1,000 tons (1)

	1913	*1920*	*1924*	*1925*	*1926*	*1927*
Netherlands	1873	3941	5882	6848	8650	9324
Spain	4016	5421	6128	6117	6276	–
British India	16468	18250	21514	21240	21258	21324
China	13776	20669	20524	20500	–	–
Japan	21316	29245	30,111	31459	29191	30460
South Africa	7984	10409	11332	11793	12458	12072
Australia	12617	13183	14108	14739	–	–

(1) Statistical Year Book for Germany, 1927.

Petroleum Produced (in 1000 tons) (1)

	1913	*1920*	*1924*	*1925*	*1926*	*1927 (2)*
Romania	1948	1109	1861	2317	3241	3976
Venezuela	–	70	1330	2885	5329	8520
Persia	248	1669	4316	4622	4667	5538
Outer India	1526	2365	2926	3066	3064	2840

(1) Statistical Year Book for Germany , 1927.
(2) Current figures given in the "Economist."

Chapter IX
Table XXIII
Industrialisation

Iron and Steel Production (in 1,000 tons). (1)

	1913	*1920*	*1924*	*1925*	*1926*
			IRON		
Italy	427	89	304	482	529
Spain	425	251	497	528	457
Hungary	190	–	116	93	188
Romania	–	19	46	64	85
Yugoslavia	–	6	15	35	–
Canada	1031	1015	629	580	749
British India	207	316	891	894	927
Japan	240	721	820	838	864
Australia	48	350	423	446	457
			STEEL		
Italy	934	774	1458	1892	1712
Spain	242	306	545	636	578
Hungary	443	62	239	231	325
Romania	140	35	87	101	–
Canada	1059	1128	670	765	789
British India	32	159	340	456	457
Japan	305	844	1098	1168	1219
Australia	14	170	311	357	366

(1) Statistical Year Book for Germany, 1927.

Chapter IX
Table XXIV
Industrialisation

Number of Cotton Spindles (in 1000).(1)

	1913	*1921*	*1924*	*1925*	*1926*
China	–	1800	3300	3350	3426
India	6084	6763	7928	8500	8510
Japan	2300	4126	4825	5292	5573
Brazil	1200	1521	1700	1950	2493
Canada	855	1100	1167	1319	1167
Mexico	700	720	802	814	830
Italy	4600	4507	4570	4771	4833
Holland	479	630	686	817	921
Portugal	480	400	503	503	503
Finland	222	240	251	253	255
Hungary	–	22	–	–	101

(1) International Statistical Annual, 1926.

Table XXV

Industialisation

Use of Machinery, 1913 and 1925 (1)

	Use in Million Mark		*As a Percentage of World Use*	
	1913	*1925*	*1913*	*1925*
Latin America	358	505	2.6	2.3
Japan	109	324	0.8	1.5
China	20	54	0.2	0.2
British India	139	225	1.0	1.0
Rest of Asia	75	76	0.5	0.4
Australia	152	292	1.1	1.3
Union of South Africa	64	99	0.5	0.4
Rest of Africa	43	68	0.3	0.3

(1) League of Nations Memorandum of the Association of German Machine Builders.

Chapter X

Table XXVI

The Great Powers of the World(1)

The following table gives a roughly accurate idea of the distribution of the world among the Great Powers and of their economic importance. We must point out that since the time to which these figures refer the share of the U.S.S.R. has considerably increased. America's leadership and China's backwardness in the sphere of production are very apparent from the figures. The figures themselves are not particularly reliable.

	Area		Population, 1924		Cultivated Land	Coal	Petroleum		
	1000 sq. km.	*per cent of Earth's Surface*	*Mill*	*Per cent of World Population*	*Mill Hectares*	*Per cent of World Reserves*	*Per cent of World Production (1925)*	*Per cent of World Reserves*	*Per cent of World Production (1925)*
British Empire	38,240	38.0	464	25.0	203(2)	22.5	26.0	18.2	1.9
U.S.A.	10,591	7.7	132	7.1	139(3)	46.0	45.3	17.0	71.3
France and Colonies	14,714	10.8	99	5.3	31(4)	1.0	5.2	2.2	–
Soviet Union	21,502	16.0	138	7.4	–	3.0	1.5	13.6	5.2
China	11,080	8.1	449	24.2	–	19.4	1.7	2.9	–
Japan	678	0.5	82	4.4	12.6	0.12	2.6	2.6	0.2
Total	96,805	71.1	1,365	73.4	–	92.02	82.3	56.5	78.6
Other Countries	39,195	28.9	489	26.6	–	7.98	17.7	43.5(5)	21.4
World	136.00 (6)	100.0	1,853	100.0	–	100.0	100.0	100.0	100.0

	Iron	Steel	Motor	Railways		Merchant Marine					
	Per cent of World Prod. (1925)	*Per cent of World Prod. (1925)*	*Driving Power 1000 h.p.*	*1000 km.*	*Per cent of World Rail-ways*	*1000 tons*	*Per cent of World Ton-nage*	*State Income $ Mill. (1924)*	*Imports Milliard $1924*	*Exports Millard $(1924)*	*Strength of Army(7) (1000)*
British Empire	11.4	10.4(8)	–	249	21.1	21,504	36.6	5,623	9.9	9.2	1,001(9)
U.S.A.	49.2	50.9	29,567	415	35.1	11,605	19.7	4,012	4.0	5.2	347
France and Colonies	13.9	10.2	6,600(0)	72	6.1	3,262	5.6	1,468	2.5	2.5	801
Soviet Union	2.0	2.1	–	60	5.1	–	–	–	0.12	0.17	600
China	0.6	0.2	–	12	1.0	–	–	490(11)	0.83	0.62	–
Japan	0.6	0.6	2,932	20	1.7	3,741	6.4	657	1.2	0.9	307
Total	77.7	74.4	–	828	70.1	40,112	68.3	–	18.55	18,59	–
Other Countries	22.3	25.6	–	352	29.9	18,673	31.7	–	8.4	6.7	–
World	100.0	100.0	–	1,180	100.0	58,785	100.0	–	27.0	35.5	–

(1) Taken from the Year Book for Economics, Politics and the Working Class Movement, 1925-26. (2) Great Britain, Ireland, Canada, India, Egypt, South Africa, Australia, New Zealand. (3) Excluding Colonies. (4) France, Algeria, Morocco, Tunis. (5) Large oilfields lie outside the immediate sphere of domination of the imperialist powers, and are the objects of continual friction and disputes (Mexico, South America, U.S.S.R., Dutch India, Persia). (6) Excluding Polar regions. (7) Including Marines. (8) Great Britain, 1907, 10,792,000. Canada, 1922, 4,774,511. (9) Only Great Britain, Australia, Canada, India, New Zealand. (10) Only France. (11) 1919.

Chapter XI

Table XXVII

The Workers' Share of Profits in the U.S.A.

In recent years the theory has been maintained in the United States, particularly by Carver, that by means of small shares and workers' shares, an important part of profits is being acquired by the workers. The complete untenableness of this assertion is demonstrated by the following table:–

The Class Distribution of Income from Profits in the U.S.A., 1924(1)

Income Group	*Number of Wage Earners*	*Per cent of Wage Earners*	*Amount of Income from Property*	*Percentage of Total Wealth*
			Milliard Dollars	
Wage Earners	27,100,000	63.0	10.0	4.3
Farmers	6,385,000	14.9	39.5	17.0
Wage Earners with income				
Below 3000$	6,755,000	15.7	26.1	11.2
from 3000-10,000$	2,500,000	5.8	57.9	25.0
over 10,000 $	260,000	0.6	98.5	42.5
Total	43,000,000	100.0	232.0	100.0

The table is drawn up on the basis of individual profit-making property and excludes property held collectively. This means that dividends and interest paid by Joint Stock Companies is included but not the internal accumulation of those Companies.

(1) Taken from "New Republic," 10/8/27.